THEMES
for early years

PEOPLE
WHO CAN HELP US

ANNE FARR & JANET MORRIS

THEMES
for early years

Authors Anne Farr and Janet Morris
Editor Sally Gray
Assistant editors Jane Bishop and Libby Russell
Series designer Lynne Joesbury
Designer Claire Belcher
Illustrations Cathy Hughes
Cover Based on an illustration by Sue Coney
Action Rhymes, Poems and Stories compiled by Jackie Andrews
Songs compiled by Peter Morrell

Designed using Aldus Pagemaker
Processed by Scholastic Ltd, Leamington Spa

Published by Scholastic Ltd, Villiers House, Clarendon Avenue, Leamington Spa, Warwickshire CV32 5PR

© 1997 Scholastic Ltd Text © 1997 Anne Farr and Janet Morris
11 12 13 14 15   3 4 5 6

The publishers gratefully acknowledge permission to reproduce the following copyright material:
Jackie Andrews for 'The Story Of The Good Samaritan' © 1997, Jackie Andrews; Clive Barnwell for 'Fireman Fred' and 'Milkman' © 1997, Clive Barnwell; Ann Bryant for 'The Wheelie Bin Song' © 1997, Ann Bryant; Debbie Campbell for 'The Driver Of The School Bus' © 1997, Debbie Campbell; Sue Cowling for 'Bakery Rhyme and 'Supermarket Sam' © 1997, Sue Cowling; John Foster for 'My Babysitter' © 1997, John Foster and 'We Must Protect The Countryside' first published in *Green Press* © 1993, John Foster (1993, Oxford University Press); Jill Harker for 'The Fireman' Poem with actions © 1997, Jill Harker; Carole Henderson Begg for 'Friends and Neighbours' © Carole Henderson Begg; Hazel Hobbs for 'Guess Who?' © 1997, Hazel Hobbs; Susanna Kendall for 'I'll Help To Cook' and 'I'll Do My Best To Help' © 1997, Susanna Kendall; Karen King for 'Susie's Specs' © 1997, Karen King; Wes Magee for 'Postie, Postie', 'Crossing The Road' and 'The Waterfall' © 1997, Wes Magee; Trevor Millum for words to the song 'Whose Hat Is That?' © 1997,Trevor Millum; Tony Mitton for 'Granny' 'Guess Who?' and 'Moving House' ('The Big Load') © 1997, Tony Mitton, Janet Morris for 'Alice And Tom Find The Way' © 1997, Janet Morris; David Moses for 'Meet My Dentist (What A Nice Man)' © 1997, David Moses; Judith Nicholls for 'The Dentist'; 'Milkman Miller' and 'Haircut' first published in *Higgledy Humbug* by Judith Nicholls © 1990, Judith Nicholls (1990, Mary Glasgow Publications now Collins Primary Poetry Pack I); Gillian Parker for the music to 'Whose Hat Is That?' © 1997, Gillian Parker; John Rice for 'Farmer' © 1997, John Rice; Geraldine Taylor for 'My Friend Billy' and 'Please Help Me Find My Rabbit' © 1997, Geraldine Taylor; Walker Books for the text of *Farmer Duck* by Martin Waddell © 1991, Martin Waddell (1991, Walker Books Ltd). Every effort has been made to trace copyright holders and the publishers apologise for any inadvertent omissions.

British Library Cataloguing-in-Publication Data A catalogue record for this book is available from the British Library.

ISBN 0-590-53463-7

The right of Anne Farr and Janet Morris to be identified as the Authors of this work has been asserted by them in accordance with the Copyright, Designs and Patents Act 1988.

CONTENTS

INTRODUCTION

The theme of 'People who help us' is a popular topic with young children and this book provides a comprehensive range of activities on the theme to help early years educators, in any setting, to plan and carry out a variety of lively activities to support this popular topic.

A young child's world is initially based on the immediate surroundings of their home. The next move is to become aware of 'people who help' in the wider world and this usually means playgroup, nursery or school. The scope of 'people who help us' then widens and in the book further activities are based around the everyday interests and routines in the children's lives.

The ideas in this book provide lively, practical and workable activities, which are suitable for use by any adults working with children of varying abilities and levels of maturity between the ages of three to six years. All the activities, while firmly rooted in structured play, are designed to prepare children for the National Curriculum and Scottish 5–14 National Guidelines. The activities also fit well into the six Areas of Learning for under-fives recommended by QCA in the document *Curriculum Guidance for the Foundation Stage*. Each activity has a specific National Curriculum subject focus but clearly learning in the early years is 'a seamless robe', and opportunities to help children develop all the skills, concepts and attitudes that are vitally important in early years education are included.

USING THEMES

There are many ways of approaching a topic on 'People who help us', and there are numerous opportunities to explore sub-themes. Chapters in this book cover the themes of people who help us in the home, in school, in health and safety, bringing our food and caring for the environment. Throughout, children are encouraged to think about people who help in the familiar environments of home and their own educational setting (school, nursery or playgroup), and then to investigate people who help us in different ways in the wider world, as individuals and as part of a community.

Many of the activities allow children to work from firsthand experience and also to build on their previous knowledge and experience. Opportunities are provided for children to discuss and explore familiar situations and to develop their own knowledge and understanding of the many people, familiar and unknown, who make considerable contributions to our lives.

CROSS-CURRICULAR LINKS

Many people working with young children choose to teach through cross-curricular themes because of the advantages presented by using an integrated approach. This method offers the opportunity for children to develop a broad range of concepts, skills and attitudes in all areas of the curriculum within an appropriate developmental context. For example, communication skills can be developed through discussion, writing, drawing, role-play, singing and modelling. Mathematical and scientific concepts can be explored as children engage in practical activities, for example, cooking, movement and building. Observational and manipulative skills should be encouraged as children create and interact with displays and investigate objects and materials. Personal and social skills will be enhanced as children work individually or collaboratively within groups and as they investigate and understand the roles of others in society.

HOW TO USE THIS BOOK

'People who help us' is one of a series of books written specifically for adults working with young children at home, in playgroups, nurseries, nursery classes or schools. The chapter entitled 'Helping at school', (Chapter 2) is intended to include playgroups or nurseries as well as school.

Within each chapter the first activity encapsulates and introduces the other activities in the chapter so that you can undertake the initial activity alone or select from the supporting activities as appropriate. The book contains material either for a long term project or for a few activities linked to other books and themes.

The content of this book has been organised to allow versatility of use, providing a complete topic pack or as an additional resource to supplement your own ideas. However you choose to use the material you can adjust the activities and resources to suit the needs of the young children in your care.

TOPIC WEB

The topic web on pages 8–9 is designed to aid planning by showing how each activity relates to the National Curriculum and Scottish 5–14 Guidelines. To ensure that the children receive a broad and balanced curriculum, the topic web has been designed with an even distribution of activities between subjects. Although each activity has been given a main subject focus most will also make important contributions to other subject areas.

For example, an activity which has been identified as having a mainly mathematical basis will often include speaking and listening and so develop language skills.

ACTIVITY PAGES

Each chapter in this section focuses on a particular theme of 'People who help us', and each individual activity is linked to a subject in the early years curriculum. For each activity a learning objective is identified which shows the main subject area and explains the purpose of the activity. A suggestion is given for the appropriate group size, but individual circumstances may influence your choice of the number of children in the group. For example, having adult helpers may mean that more children can participate in the activity than is suggested. A list of materials and equipment needed before the activity can begin is provided and any preparatory work necessary such as making or setting out equipment is listed. If the children need to have had previous experience or knowledge which is essential to the success of the activity this is also mentioned.

Step-by-step instructions are outlined on how to introduce each activity and guidance is offered on what the children should do. Although explicit instructions are given, a certain amount of flexibility is required and most of the activities can be adapted for different ability levels.

The main discussion points are identified, though it is important to adopt a flexible approach and allow children to lead the conversation into other, equally valid areas. Some activities involve adult intervention throughout, while others may lend themselves to a summary discussion after the activity has been carried out. Whenever possible, encourage the children to share their ideas with a friend, an older child or an adult helper as well as yourself.

Follow-up ideas for extending each activity, both within the subject and its associated areas are also listed. Be prepared to follow up ideas which the children suggest, even if it moves the topic into a slightly different area than you had originally planned. It is important to give children the opportunity to experience self-directed tasks.

DISPLAY

Ideas for how to set up stimulus displays linked to the various themes of 'People who help us' are provided. A list of the materials required, instructions on how to assemble the display and points for discussion are covered. Most of the displays are interactive and whenever possible you can encourage the children to help collect and select resources and to assemble the display. Always allocate plenty of time for the children to examine the displays individually and organise a group or class discussion time to talk about them.

ASSEMBLIES

This chapter provides ideas for planning assemblies or group sharing times related to the theme. Each assembly has its own practical ideas on how the children can be encouraged to contribute, to reflect on the specific theme and a relevant prayer and song are suggested

RESOURCES

A useful selection of stories, poems, action rhymes and songs linked with the 'People who help us' topic are given in this section. Much of the material is new and has been specially commissioned to complement the topic. All of these resources are photocopiable.

PHOTOCOPIABLE SHEETS

Eight photocopiable pages each linking with a specific activity detailed earlier in the book are provided. Make sure that the children understand how to carry out the activity, and that any new vocabulary is fully explained before you hand out the sheets. Allow time to discuss the completed sheet with each child in order to assess how much they have understood.

RECOMMENDED MATERIALS

Details of story-books, information books, poetry and songs linked to the topic are listed on the final page. Encourage the children to bring in their own favourite stories, poems and songs which focus on 'People who help us' to share with your group.

EXPRESSIVE ARTS

Planning towards the National Curriculum and the Scottish National guidelines 5-14

THEMES *for early years*

PPLE
HELP US

PHOTOCOPIABLE

PREPARING FOR PRIMARY SCHOOL

Curriculum provides an overall programme of study for each subject and requires teachers to assess the level of attainment of each child at the end of the Key Stage. The assessment is carried out partly through nationwide testing but it is mainly the teacher's professional judgement that determines the overall level in each subject that a child has attained.

By the time children begin Level One, they will need to have developed essential learning skills. These include communication, observation, social skills and physical skills.

The activities suggested in this book allow for the vital skills to be developed through firsthand experience. The topic web on pages 8–9 also shows how the learning objective of each activity relates to the subjects of the National Curriculum.

THE SCOTTISH 5–14 GUIDELINES

In Scotland, there are National Guidelines for schools on what should be taught to children between the ages of five to fourteen.

These National Guidelines are divided into six main curriculum areas: English Language, Mathematics, Environmental Studies, Expressive Arts, Religious and Moral Education, and Personal and Social Development.

Within these main areas, further subjects are found – for example, 'Expressive Arts' also includes art and design, drama, music and PE. Strands are also identified within each subject – for example, Mathematics includes Problem-solving and enquiry and Shape, position and movement.

Most nurseries will find that the experiences they are offering will provide a good foundation for this curriculum. The activities in this book have been specially written to prepare for many aspects of it, and they will also fit well into the pre-five curriculum guidelines issued by local authorities throughout Scotland.

We have organised the activities into separate areas of the curriculum on the topic web on pages 8–9 to help you with your planning. The children's personal and social development is an on-going theme that is incorporated throughout the activities in this book.

Early years children are individuals and will be at different stages of development. Whatever level they have reached, it is important to help prepare a sound foundation from which all children can go on to study the subjects of the National Curriculum. This can be achieved through many everyday play activities.

The National Curriculum was established to standardise the subjects and subject content, taught at all levels of a child's education. It is intended that any child will be able to go to a school throughout the country and find the same areas of the curriculum being covered for the same amount of time every week. The National Curriculum subjects are: English, mathematics, science, history, geography, design and technology, ICT, art and design, music and PE.

Most of the activities suggested in this topic are based on common play activities such as role-play, drawing, using construction toys or making models. However, each activity also has a specific learning objective: to develop important skills in preparation for the first stage of the National Curriculum.

TOWARDS LEVEL ONE

The requirements of the National Curriculum do not apply until children start Year 1. The National

CHAPTER 1
HELPING AT HOME

Children's experiences begin in the home. Their first knowledge of people helping comes from the things that they observe in their home setting. Many children love to play at 'helping' — washing the dishes, going shopping and cleaning the car. This chapter explores the ways that people help at home.

WHO HELPS IN OUR HOME?

Objective

Maths — To help children sort and classify, recognise and order numbers.

Group size

Introduce the activity to the whole group, then work with six to ten children.

What you need

Photocopiable sheet on page 88, the home corner furnished with appropriate equipment (table, chairs, cooker, bed, pram, vacuum cleaner, dusters, brooms, tea-cloths, tea-set). Felt-tipped pens.

Preparation

Be sensitive to each child's home situation so that no embarrassing questions or comments are put to the child. Make photocopies of the activity sheet, one for each child.

What to do

Group children around the home corner. Ask them to identify things they see in the home (sink, cooker, tables, chairs, baby's cot). Ask the children who lives in their home.

Encourage the children to think about work that needs doing at home. Who cooks the food, washes the dishes, cleans the home, tidies up the toys, baby-sits and so on? Ask the children how they help. Explain that other people may come to help (grandad, aunts and child-minders).

Show the children the photocopiable sheet and explain to them that they need to draw people who live at home that help in one column and people who come to their homes in order to help in the other column.

Discussion

Gather the children into a group and look at each child's sheet. Count and classify: 'Karen has drawn five people who come to her home to help'. Ask the children to say who they are and what they do.

Follow-up activities

✧ Mount the data sheets on bright backing paper. Make a wall display with any pictures or posters that were used in the introduction. Write captions: 'Some people who help us live in our home'; 'Some people visit and help'.
✧ Carry out a mapping activity matching person to job.
✧ Suggest that the children write or dictate a list of ways they have helped at home over a short period of time (a weekend or week).

CLEANING DAY

Objective

Science – To encourage children to appreciate the need for hygiene in the home.

Group size

Six to eight children.

What you need

A toy washing machine or a large box decorated to represent a washing machine, a small washing basket, items of laundry (clothing, towels, tea-towels), play iron, ironing board, toy sink, plastic bucket, warm water, cleaning cloth, feather duster, liquid cleaner, spray polish, duster, plastic plates, beakers, bottle of mild washing-up liquid, small table, small pot of mixed powder paint, large piece of sugar paper, thick felt-tipped pen.

Preparation

Set up the role-play area as a home. Collect the cleaning materials and washing basket with dirty laundry. Check that none of the children have allergies to soap products.

What to do

Show the children a 'dirty plate' and ask the children how it might be cleaned. Choose someone to wash the plate. Encourage the children to think about the sequence of events needed to wash up: add the washing-up liquid; insert the dish cloth into the water; immerse the plate; wash the plate; dry the plate.

Show the children the washing basket and examine the soiled clothes. How do we get our clothes clean? Encourage the children to identify things which would be put in a washing machine. Allow one child at a time to place items inside the 'play' washing machine. How are clothes dried? (Outside on a washing line, in tumble dryers at the laundrette.) How do we get the crinkles out of clothes?

Introduce the idea of a 'Cleaning Day' for the role-play area. Ask the children what else should be cleaned? Demonstrate by cleaning paint marks off a small table. Encourage the children to think of other things in the home that need cleaning (carpets, furniture, windows). Make a list of cleaning jobs for the role-play area.

Enlist the children's help to clean the home corner. Encourage them to tick the cleaning list as jobs are complete. Ensure that both boys and girls are involved in all the cleaning activities to avoid gender stereotyping.

Discussion

Encourage the children to consider why it is important to have clean clothes and a clean home. What are germs? What do they do? How can we remove them?

Follow-up activities

✧ Organise the children into pairs to create washing machines from junk boxes.
✧ Create a wall display using a real or a drawn clothes line. Ask the children to draw or paint laundry and peg it on the line.
✧ Discuss safety in the home (cleaning products, electrical equipment).

ALICE AND TOM'S CHILD-MINDER

Objective

Geography — To encourage early mapping skills.

Group size

Up to six children.

What you need

The story 'Alice and Tom find the way' in the Resources on page 80, photocopiable sheet on page 89 for each child, a large plan of a kitchen showing the position of kitchen furniture and equipment, felt-tipped pens and crayons.

Preparation

Gather the children together and read the story 'Alice and Tom show the way' to them.

What to do

After the story ask the children the following questions: Why did Emma come to look after Alice and Tom? Why did the children need a special map?

Ask the children if they can think of any other maps or plans that Mum might have given to Emma. Suggest a plan of the kitchen showing where everything is kept. Show the children the prepared kitchen plan and encourage them to identify the different features.

Show the children the photocopiable sheet of Alice and Tom's journey to school. Ask them to trace the route to Alice and Tom's school. Encourage them to identify the places on the map (Oliver's house, library, corner shop, railway station). Ask the children to think of the people Emma, Alice and Tom met and where they joined them.

Discussion

Talk about the role of a child-minder. Do the children know someone who helps look after children (encourage the children who are looked after by child-minders to contribute from their own experiences). Why did Mum give a map to Emma to take the children to school? Who did they meet on their way? How many people set off from Alice and Tom's house? How many people arrived at school together?

Follow-up activities

✧ Invite the children to draw and paint pictures of Alice, Tom and Emma on their way to school.
✧ Make a wall display of the route to the playgroup/ nursery, child-minders or school. Label the places familiar to the children.
✧ Read the poem 'My babysitter' in the Resources section on page 70.
✧ Let the children make a plan of your room and label it.

MOVING HOUSE

Objective

PE – To use movement to represent a story based on a family moving home.

Group size

Any size.

What you need

A large open space, a tambourine.

Preparation

Ask if any of the children have moved to a different home. Discuss what happens when somebody moves home. Read the poem 'Moving House' in the resources section on page 67.

What to do

Read the simple story (below) to the children and suggest some movements to go with it:

> The Jones family are moving to a new house. They are going to be very busy!
>
> A removal person arrives to look at the contents to be moved, bringing boxes and tea chests to be packed. The family starts to pack.
>
> On the moving day the removal people take out the furniture and put it in the van.
>
> The Jones family arrive at their new home and the removal people begin to carry in the furniture, boxes and tea chests.
>
> The family excitedly unpack everything. They have to be careful not to break anything and they need to work as a team, passing things to each other and putting them away gently. Some things are big and heavy and other things are fragile and difficult to carry.
>
> The children in the family are excited and move around with quick and happy movements, exploring all the rooms and looking in the cupboards, under the stairs and behind doors.

Use the tambourine, in different ways, to accompany the children's movements and as a signal to start and stop moving. Allow the children to work individually and in small groups.

Discussion

Discuss how the removal people in the story helped the family to move. How did the people in the family help each other? How will you carry and move different household objects? (A box of crockery, a large settee, a tall cupboard.) How much space do you need? Which direction will you move in? Are you working quickly, slowly, gently, strongly? Are you working by yourself or with somebody? Can you help each other to carry something long and heavy? Can you lift something huge but light?

Follow-up activities

✧ Complete the photocopiable sheet, 'Moving house' on page 90.
✧ Make a template of a removal van and cut one out for each child. Ask the children to cut out pictures of people, furniture and household goods from catalogues. Invite them to stick these in place in the van. Reinforce positional words such as: above, beside, under, on top and below.
✧ Encourage the children to tell their own moving house stories.
✧ Wrap a few familiar objects (a teapot, stool and teddy) and ask the children to identify them.

HELPING IN THE GARDEN

Objective

Music — To explore sounds made from natural objects and make simple instruments which can be used to accompany familiar songs and rhymes.

Group size

Up to six children to make simple instruments. Larger groups to use the instruments to accompany the songs and rhymes.

What you need

Pictures or photographs of gardens at different times of the year. Seed catalogues and gardening magazines. A selection of dried peas, beans and other suitable seeds. Various containers (yoghurt cartons, cardboard rolls, plastic bottles). Different sorts of brightly coloured paper (wrapping paper, tissue paper, sugar paper), elastic bands, adhesive tape, felt-tipped pens.

Preparation

Choose appropriate pictures or photographs of gardens and mount these onto backing paper. Collect seed catalogues and gardening magazines. Assemble a selection of different seeds. Remind the children of the dangers of putting small items in their mouths. Explain that seeds and berries should not be tasted as some types can make them very ill.

What to do

Group the children on the carpet and show the photographs or pictures of gardens. Ask them what they can see in the gardens (flowers, vegetables, grass, garden ornaments, ponds, seats, sheds, tools).

Show the seed catalogues. Explain that gardeners choose seeds to plant in their gardens so that they will have different vegetables and flowers. Show the children the seeds and encourage them to observe the differences.

Write labels for the seeds and place a picture of what they will grow into by their side.

Assemble the containers, different paper, adhesive, elastic bands, felt-tipped pens and seeds on the table. Place some seeds in a plastic container.

Shake the 'instrument' for the children to hear the sound. Encourage the children to choose from the materials and seeds to create their instruments. They may need help to secure the seeds inside the instruments. Invite the children to decorate their instruments using the felt-tipped pens. Make sure each child's instrument is clearly named.

Discussion

Ask the children if they know anybody who has a garden. (Be aware that some children may not have gardens of their own.) What happens in the garden during the year? (Draw attention to the photographs or pictures.) What jobs need to be done? Do the children help in the garden? What do they do? (Perhaps weeding, picking vegetables, raking up the leaves, digging.)

Follow-up activities

✧ Collect a set of garden tools, a wheelbarrow, seed trays and plant pots, labels and a watering can, and display them in the room. Encourage children to touch and examine them, and consider how they are used.
✧ Say the nursery rhyme 'Mary, Mary, quite contrary' and try to learn it.

GRAN AND GRANDAD COME TO HELP

Objective

History – To help children become aware of the passing of time represented by three generations of their family.

Group size

Six to ten children.

What you need

A copy of *Do you know what Grandad did?* by Brian Smith (Orchard Picture books). A number of photographs showing older people who are grandparents. A photograph or picture showing three generations of a family, for example the Royal family. Sugar paper and pastels or chalk.

Preparation

Read the story *Do you know what Grandad did?* (a story about a grandad who looks after the children when mum is out, but gets many things wrong). Ask the children to recall how grandad tries to help.

Show the children photographs and pictures of grandparents, and the family picture with three generations. Ask them to bring in photographs of their own grandparents (be sensitive to individual children's circumstances).

What to do

Ask each child to describe a way in which their grandparents help. Make some suggestions (looking after you when mum and dad are out, doing the ironing and so on). Help the children to think of ideas for themselves. Give each child a large sheet of sugar paper and coloured pastels or chalks. Ask them to draw their ideas of how gran and grandad help in the home.

Discussion

Encourage each child to talk about his or her picture. Discuss the relationship between their parents and their grandparents. Explain that when children grow up and have a family their parents become grandparents. Some children may have great-grandparents. Ask if they have a great-gran and great-grandad.

Follow-up activities

✧ Mount the display of grandparents and family photographs on the wall including the children's photographs.
✧ Stick all the children's pastel/chalk drawings in a large book. Ask each child to suggest a caption for his or her picture with an adult acting as scribe, for example: 'This is my Gran putting me to bed'. Read the completed book to the group. Allow time for the children to 'read' it themselves.
✧ Arrange for a gran or grandad to visit and help with an activity.

NEIGHBOURS LEND A HAND

Objective

RE – To discuss ways people can help each other.

Group size

Any size.

What you need

A simple version of the story of *The Good Samaritan* (see page 74 of the Resources section), picture of a street scene, a large sheet of paper, felt-tipped pens, small pieces of drawing paper, pencils, crayons, glue sticks.

Preparation

Find a poster or large picture of a street scene showing different homes.

Write the caption: 'Our neighbours help' in the middle of the large sheet of paper so that arrows may be drawn outwards. Assemble the drawing and writing materials required for the children's activity. Display the book or story of *The Good Samaritan* on a nearby table or cupboard top.

What to do

Retell the story of *The Good Samaritan* choosing children to play the parts of the various characters. Emphasise the point that the man needed help but not everybody wanted to help him.

Show the picture of the street and discuss the word neighbour. Ask the children if they have neighbours. Talk about people who may live nearby and not just next door. Suggest that neighbours sometimes help us, for example: feed the pets when we are out; lend us things that we need; collect or take children to school, nursery, the child-minders or playgroup. Ask the children if they have neighbours who sometimes help.

On the prepared sheet of paper write small labels from the arrows describing how neighbours help, using the children's suggestions. Invite the children to draw and colour pictures of their neighbour and stick these near the appropriate caption.

Discussion

Tell the children that the story that they have heard is from The Bible. Explain that the Good Samaritan was a good neighbour and wanted to help the man. Suggest that the children are neighbours and can help each other during the day. Ask the children how they can help each other, for example, by sharing crayons, helping each other to get changed at PE and playing games together.

Follow-up activities

✧ Learn the song 'When I needed a neighbour', from '*Someone's Singing Lord*' (A&C Black).
✧ Make a list of ways the children can help their neighbours in the group. Record ways of helping over a short period of time.
✧ Describe ways that people help each other throughout the world (Children in Need, Red Nose Day). Use Red Nose Day or a similar fund-raising idea such as a nursery rhyme character theme day, or a sponsored activity, to encourage children to participate in helping those in need.

POSTING LETTERS

Objective

English — To encourage early writing skills.

Group size

Up to six children.

What you need

The story of *The Jolly Postman* by Janet and Allan Ahlberg, (Heinemann). Notepaper in various colours and shapes, a variety of new and used envelopes, circulars, catalogues, a postman's hat, a large bag or satchel, a toy postbox, thick pencils, crayons, Blu-Tack and mounting paper.

Preparation

Read the story of *The Jolly Postman*, which is about a postman delivering letters to some familiar characters from well-known stories. Find out what time post is collected from the nearest pillar-box and take the children for a walk to watch the postman/woman emptying the letters into the sack.

What to do

Group the children on the carpet and talk about what they saw at the pillar-box.

Show some of the used envelopes pointing out the name, address, stamp and post mark and a selection of post that might come to any home (birthday card, personal letter, bills, holiday postcard, a circular).

What happens to the letters once they are posted? (The postman/woman will take them to the sorting office where they will be sorted into areas ready for delivery). Ask the children to find out what time the postman comes to their home.

Organise the children into pairs and suggest each child writes a letter to their partner telling him/her about something important (a birthday/festival, a new baby, a holiday, a special toy). Give out note-paper, pencils and crayons. Very young children can make a drawing to show their ideas or ask an adult to act as scribe.

Encourage the children to post their letters. Choose someone to act as post person (wearing the hat and carrying the postbag). He/she can empty the postbox and deliver the letters.

Discussion

Encourage the children to think about the different mail people receive. What mail do they receive? (Postcards, invitations, greeting cards.) What time does the post person come? Where does he/she put the mail? Can people send messages in other ways? (Fax, telephone, smoke signals, sign language.)

Follow-up activities

✧ Set up a letter writing area in the room for the children to use when they have free choice. Provide a variety of different sized and coloured paper, various envelopes, post cards (plain and printed), pencils, felt-tipped pens, crayons, toy stamps, glue sticks and a postbox.
✧ Collect a selection of different sized used envelopes (plain, coloured, business, air mail). Encourage the children to sort these in different ways (size, colour, shape, stamps).
✧ Learn the song 'Guess Who?' in the Resources section on page 82.

CHAPTER 2
HELPING AT SCHOOL

As children start playgroup, nursery or school their horizons broaden and they encounter a wider range of 'people who help us'. In this chapter we will look closely at the people they may encounter in this new environment.

WHO HELPS IN OUR GROUP?

Objective

English – To encourage children to talk about the different people involved in their learning environment and the ways they help.

Group size

Various.

What you need

Camera and film, large piece of paper, board or easel, white card or stiff paper, Blu-Tack, thick felt-tipped pens, three large hoops of different colours.

Preparation

Take photographs of all the people who are involved in helping at the school/playgroup/nursery (secretary, play-leader, cleaner, dinner supervisor and so on).

Prepare a large piece of paper with the caption 'People who help us in school/nursery/playgroup' and display it on a board or easel. Make labels saying: 'People who help in our room'; 'People who help outside the room' and 'People who help in and out of the room'.

What to do

Show the children the paper with the caption, 'People who help us in school ...'. Ask them to think of all the different people who help at school. Show them the photographs one at a time. Ask the children to name the people and explain their role. Write the helpers' names and how they help in a list on the paper.

Place the large hoops on the floor. Show the children the labels (described in 'Preparation') and place a label in each hoop. Sort the photographs by encouraging the children to think and discuss whether the person helps in the classroom, out of the classroom or does both. The children may not associate people such as the cleaner with helping in the classroom.

Discussion

Ask the children to describe some of the things they have seen the people who help them in school/playgroup/nursery doing. Were they surprised about any of the things that they found out?

Follow-up activities

✧ Make a 'People who help us' book. Name the person and say how he/she helps (the lollipop person helps me cross the road; the secretary types letters to send to our parents; the premises officer opens the building in the morning).
✧ Play a game of 'Guess who?' with an adult describing the activity and the children guessing who does it. For example: I make sure all the windows are locked at night and open the doors in the morning. Answer – the premises officer.

ON PATROL

Objective

Geography – To learn and understand about road safety by observing the lollipop person and through discussion.

Group size

Any size.

What you need

A picture or poster of a lollipop person on duty.

Preparation

Find a poster or picture of a lollipop person. Invite a lollipop person to visit the group to talk to the children and show their uniform and lollipop stick.

What to do

Show the children the picture or poster of the lollipop person. Encourage them to name the person, describe her role and identify the various parts of the uniform and the lollipop stick. Ask the children where they see a lollipop person.

Talk about the way in which the lollipop person helps us keep safe. Explain that they should never cross the road without an adult. Emphasise the need to look for the lollipop person, to listen to what she says, and to watch what she does to help us cross the road safely. Explain the importance of the crossing patrol lights.

Discussion

Why is it important to find a safe place to cross the road? Where does the lollipop person stand? How do we recognise the lollipop person? How does she help you cross the road safely? Encourage the children to think about the traffic. Discuss what drivers need to do when they see the crossing patrol lights and the lollipop person giving instructions.

Follow-up activities

✧ Read the poem 'Crossing the road' in the Resources section on page 71.
✧ Take the children into a large space and practice crossing the road safely. Ask a lollipop person to be involved.
✧ Make a large class model of a lollipop person using boxes, painting the uniform and making the lollipop stick.
✧ Take some photographs of the local lollipop person carrying out her job and display these in a prominent place.
✧ Encourage the children to role-play using a play road mat. Include toy transport, models of children, adults and a lollipop person.

WHAT CAN WE DO?

Objective

RE - To enable children to become more responsible for their own setting and to encourage them to help others.

Group size

Whole class or group; smaller groups.

What you need

A collection of objects that have been left out or on the floor the previous day, large piece of paper, thick felt-tipped pen, dustpan, brush, waste-paper bin, crayon tin, a large cardboard box, a couple of plastic containers.

Preparation

Write a caption saying 'What can we do?' on the paper and a label saying 'Lost property' to stick on the box. Collect objects left out the previous day and place them in a container. Assemble the dustpan, brush and other containers.

What to do

Explain to the children the roles of the premises officer and cleaners and talk about the special jobs they do (mopping floors, vacuuming carpets, emptying litter bins).

Show the children the objects. Tell them that these were left out. Suggest that if everybody tidied up, the cleaners and premises officer would be able to carry out their special work more easily.

Select some objects. Ask the children where the objects belong. Invite them to return these to their proper places and to use the dustpan and brush to sweep up any mess on the floor. Suggest the children play their part in keeping the room tidy to help the premises officer and cleaners. Display the paper and read the caption 'What can we do?' Write 'sensible' suggestions on the list.

At the end of the day remind children of the 'What can we do?' list. Suggest that the children can help in other areas of the building and outside too!

Discussion

What happens when we all go home? Who makes the room clean and tidy for the next day? What happens to objects left on the floor? How can we help the cleaners and premises officers? Ask the children for suggestions (place crisp packets in the litter bin, put lost clothes in the 'lost property' box, pick objects off the floor and sort them into the appropriate containers).

Follow-up activities

✧ Make a count of objects found on the floor. Compare with the number from the previous day.
✧ Find the location of litter bins around the educational setting.
✧ Design a self assessment sheet to show what the children can do to help. For example, I can ... sort the crayons, put my coat on the peg, leave my clothes tidy when I do PE.
✧ Teach the children to sing the song 'Milk bottle tops and paper bags' in *Someone's Singing Lord*, (A&C Black).

A BUSY DAY

Objective

Mathematics – To introduce 'time' vocabulary and to develop sequencing for periods of time during the day.

Group size

Up to six children at a time.

What you need

Co-operation from the secretary to allow the children to visit the office and see him or her at work. If you don't have a secretary in your setting, base the activity on the day in the life of one of the helpers at playgroup or nursery. A diary with some entries (new parents visiting, open day, holiday). Large pieces of paper, pencils, felt-tipped pens, crayons.

Preparation

Fold the paper into quarters to make each child their own zigzag book. Write a caption: 'A busy day' on the front page. The following pages should have captions for the periods: morning, lunch-time, afternoon, home-time. Invite the secretary to talk about her role. Make a list of activities that can be used to help the children develop sequencing and understand periods of the day (opening the mail in the morning, making the coffee at break-time, answering the phone at lunch-time, typing letters to go in the afternoon post, delivering messages before home-time).

What to do

Suggest that the children are going to have a 'busy day'. Ask the children if they know the name of the secretary. Encourage them to think about the secretary's role. Explain that they are going to visit the secretary to see and hear what she/he does. Take the children to the office.

Invite the secretary to show some of the equipment that she/he uses at work, such as the word processor for writing letters, the telephone for taking and making calls, the visitors' book and the diary.

Ask the children to make a 'busy day' zigzag book for the secretary. Suggest they draw a picture of the secretary on the cover. Focus the children's attention on some of the jobs carried out by the secretary during different parts of the day. Encourage the children to illustrate these on each page. Ask an adult to act as scribe to write their captions.

Discussion

What is the name of the secretary? When have the children met the secretary? Explain that the secretary is there to help everybody — children, adults, people inside the building and people from outside. What equipment does the secretary use?

Follow-up activities

✧ Set up an office in the role-play area with typewriter, stationery, telephone and other office equipment.
✧ Encourage the children to deliver messages to the secretary, so they become familiar with the office environment.

LUNCH-TIME

Objective

Science —To encourage healthy eating through a balanced diet.

Group size

Whole group or class.

What you need

The co-operation of the school cook to talk about his/her role (or another nutritionist/parent if you don't have a school cook). A painting easel or display board covered with a large sheet of white paper, thick felt-tipped pens (orange, red and green), photocopiable sheet 'My healthy meal' on page 91, crayons, felt-tipped pens.

Preparation

Arrange for the cook to visit the children. Set up the easel, write the caption: 'Our favourite foods'. Make a photocopy of the activity sheet (page 91) for each child.

What to do

Gather the children on the carpet. Introduce the cook/nutritionist and invite him to explain his role (choosing daily menu, ordering supplies, preparing and cooking the food). Encourage the cook to show his uniform and explain the importance of hygiene.

Ask the children to name their favourite foods. Write these on the sheet. Talk about healthy foods. Draw a green coloured ring round healthy foods, an orange ring round the less healthy, and red round the least healthy (these colours link to traffic lights).

Suggest the children plan their own healthy meal using the photocopiable sheet on page 91. Encourage them to draw their food and drink in the appropriate place and invite them to label their healthy meals with an adult acting as scribe if necessary.

Discussion

Why do we need to eat healthy food? What is your favourite meal? How does the cook choose the menu? What food do we eat most days? What foods taste nice but are not very healthy? What are your favourite treats? Why do our bodies need different foods? Why do cooks wear uniforms?

Follow-up activities

✧ Play 'I went to the supermarket and I bought ...' with each child repeating the list that went before and adding a new item.
✧ Set up the role-play area as a café with tables and chairs, plastic food, plates, cutlery, menus and uniforms for a cook, chef, waiter and waitress.
✧ Look at, smell and sample food from other cultures (be aware of any allergies and warn the children that the food may be hot).

MY HELPER

Objective

Art - To develop close observational drawing skills.

Group size

Six to eight children.

What you need

A collection of prints or pictures showing people, painted by artists at different times, such as Rembrandt and Beryl Cook. Large sheets of sugar paper, pastels.

Preparation

Ask someone who comes to be a helper if they would be willing to participate in the activity. Show the prints or pictures to the children. Draw the children's attention to hair length, colour and styles, facial features, clothing and any other important aspects. Explain to the children that they are going to make 'portraits' of someone they know.

What to do

Ask the chosen helper to be the 'artist's model'. Describe the appearance of the 'model' pointing out the visual aspects that were discussed from the prints or pictures.

Give each child a sheet of paper. Ask what colour pastels they will need for the hair, face and clothing of the 'model'. Help the children to appreciate the size proportions of the model. Give each child as much individual help as necessary until each child has finished their 'portrait'.

Discussion

How can you tell it is a picture of your helper? If you make a portrait of someone what things do you have to look carefully at? How is a portrait different from a photograph?

Follow-up activities

✧ Make a wall display of the portraits with 'cut-out' frames. Write a descriptive caption, suggested by the children and written by the adult, explaining who the portrait shows and what the 'helper' does.
✧ Take the children to a local gallery to see original portraits.
✧ Show the children a selection of famous portraits in magazines, books, on postcards, or on the CD-ROM 'Art Gallery' (Microsoft).

SPICK AND SPAN

Objective

Science — To encourage understanding of how cleaning equipment works.

Group size

Up to eight children.

What you need

The help of the group or school premises officer/cleaner in charge. Access to cleaning equipment (a vacuum cleaner, electric floor polisher, broom, dustpan and brush, dusters, polish, mops, buckets and disinfectant), old mail order catalogues or magazines showing cleaning equipment, a large sheet of paper, scissors, glue sticks and brushes.

Preparation

Ask the premises officer or cleaner in charge to explain to the children what work they do when the children have gone home. Collect the cleaning equipment. Draw a line down the middle of the large sheet of paper. Write captions saying: 'Worked by electricity' and 'Not worked by electricity' above the columns.

What to do

Gather the children together and encourage them to recall what the premises officer/cleaner in charge has told and shown them. Explain that some of the equipment works by electricity and some does not. Ask the children if they can identify which things need electricity. Place the items of cleaning equipment into two sets — those that work by electricity and those that do not work by electricity.

Give the children the mail order catalogues and magazines and suggest they cut out the items of cleaning equipment they can find. When they have collected a few items encourage them to sort the pictures into the two sets previously discussed and place the items on the large sheet of paper. Check these are in the right column. Help the children to stick these down.

Gather the children together and look at the chart. Reinforce the language 'works by electricity' and 'does not work by electricity'.

Discussion

What does the premises officer/cleaner use to clean the floor? Invite the children to suggest the best equipment and ways of cleaning different areas (the floor, carpet, table tops, window ledges, windows, sinks and toilets). What would happen if the building was never cleaned? Why do we have to be careful with things that use electricity? Take the opportunity to discuss safety when using electrical items and when using cleaning materials (strong disinfectant or polish).

Follow-up activities

◇ Make a collage to show the premises officer or cleaner carrying out different cleaning jobs. Use a variety of different materials and textures.
◇ Encourage the children to think of ways they can help the premises officer and cleaners keep the building clean.
◇ Ask the children to find other pictures of things in the home that use electricity.

A VISIT TO THE LIBRARY

Objective

English – To encourage children to use the local library and develop an enjoyment of books.

Group size

Introduction with large group/whole class. Six to ten children at a time for the main activity.

What you need

A collection of interesting, well illustrated, children's fiction and information books, small pieces of card (to represent library tickets), rubber date stamp, ink pad, posters of books, paper, pens, paper-clips.

Preparation

Invite the local children's librarian to visit and read a selection of stories and poems to the children. Ask the librarian to talk about his job in the library.

Arrange a visit to the local library. Encourage the children to observe the librarian at work (inspecting and issuing library cards, returning books to shelves and so on). Invite each group of children to choose a book and observe how they are issued.

What to do

Change the role-play area into a library. Put up the book posters. Encourage the children to choose books from around the setting and those chosen during the library visit to place in the library. Choose a book to read to the whole group.

Insert a blank sheet of paper in each book (held by paper-clip). Using the prepared library tickets and the date stamp, allow two children at a time to act as librarians and the rest of the group as clients.

Discussion

Who goes to the library? Who chooses the books? What does the librarian do? Why does the librarian put a date in the library books? How are story books different from information books? What are the children's favourite stories? When would we look for information in books?

Follow-up activities

◇ Set up a story-writing project with an adult acting as scribe. Make this into a large home-made book, using word processing where possible. Encourage children to illustrate aspects of the story. Display the finished books in the library area.
◇ Organise a 'book week' and ask other adults to come and read stories/books. Invite the children to dress up as their favourite character from a story.

CHAPTER 3
KEEPING US HEALTHY

As children grow and develop they encounter a range of health professionals: the dentist, doctor and school nurse for example. This chapter explores the roles of people who help the children to 'keep healthy'.

WHAT CAN WE HEAR?

Objective

Science — To enable children to understand the importance of hearing.

Group size

The whole group or class.

What you need

An audio cassette of common everyday sounds, (an alarm clock going off, water coming out of the tap, a telephone ringing, a washing machine working). Painting easel covered in a sheet of light coloured paper, thick felt-tipped pen. The assistance of the visiting audiometrist / school nurse to talk to the children and show their equipment if possible.

Preparation

Take the children on a 'listening' walk. Focus on two contrasting environments: a busy noisy area, such as a high street; and a quiet area, such as a park. Put the children in small groups with an adult.

What to do

After the walk gather the group together on the carpet. Ask the children to recall some of the sounds they heard during the busy and quiet parts of their walk. List these sounds under the heading: 'Sounds we heard on our listening walk'. Separate the noisy and quiet sounds into two columns.

On another occasion play a 'familiar sounds' tape. Ask the children to identify each sound. Write down the sounds they hear into two different categories: 'Sounds we like hearing' and 'Sounds we do not like to hear'. Ask the children to place their hands over their ears and play the tape again. What sounds did they hear?

If possible invite an audiometrist to come and explain the role and the equipment used.

Discussion

What sounds do you like to hear? Why do you like those sounds? What sounds don't you like to hear? Why? Explain that some people have poor or no hearing and are deaf. Encourage the children to imagine what it must be like to have little or no hearing. Show them a hearing aid and ask the children what it does. Talk about the audiometrist and explain how they try to help people.

Follow-up activities

✧ Collect pictures of various animals and discuss the position of their ears.
✧ Make a listening corner and encourage children to listen to and tape sounds.
✧ Read and dramatise the poem 'Guess who' in the Resources section on page 72.

CHECK-UP AT THE DENTIST'S

Objective

Science — To develop an awareness of how the dentist helps us to keep our teeth healthy.

Group size

Any size.

What you need

Photograph or picture of a dentist, a dental appointment card, diary or calendar, toothbrush, toothpaste, a chair and plastic apron, dental hygiene posters and pamphlets.

Preparation

Collect a dental appointment card to show the children. Write down a time for the visit and make a note of it in the diary or on the calendar. Ask your own dentist if it is possible to have a photograph of him or her in uniform. Enquire if it is possible to have a sample of children's and adults' teeth. Purchase a child's toothbrush and toothpaste. Collect dental hygiene posters and pamphlets suitable for young children.

What to do

Show the children your diary or calendar and ask them why you might use one. Show them the dental appointment card with the date and time explaining that it is time for you to visit the dentist.

Explain that the dentist helps us to keep our teeth healthy. Emphasise that people don't just go to the dentist when their teeth hurt but we need to go for regular check-ups.

Show the children the photograph or picture of the dentist. Explain that the dentist wears special clothes, and a special mask and gloves. Talk about what happens when you visit the dentist for a check-up.

Ask the children to imagine they are visiting the dentist. Place the chair in front of the group. Choose two children to participate as patient and dental nurse, with you acting as the dentist.

Carry out a short and simple role-play of the dental nurse bringing the patient in to see the dentist. Make the child welcome. Ask the child to sit in the chair and encourage the dental nurse to put the plastic apron around the patient. Ask the patient to 'open wide' and pretend to examine his or her teeth. Make positive comments about looking after teeth properly by regular brushing and not eating too many sweet things.

Show the children the new toothbrush and toothpaste and explain the correct way to clean teeth.

Discussion

Ask the children if they have ever been to the dentist. What did they do when they arrived at the dentist? Does their dentist wear special clothes? Do other people help him or her? Why does the dentist need a special chair and special tools?

Follow-up activities

✧ Make a graph to show the colour of children's toothbrushes.
✧ Sing 'Meet my dentist (what a nice man)' in the Resources section on page 81.
✧ Read the poem 'The dentist' in the Resources section on page 67.
✧ Make the role-play area into the dentist's waiting room and surgery.

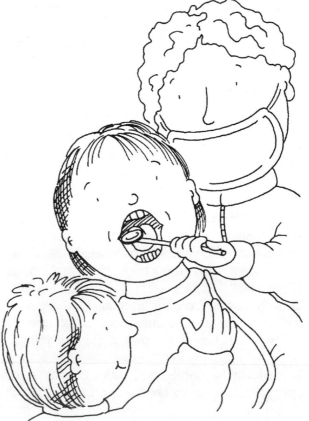

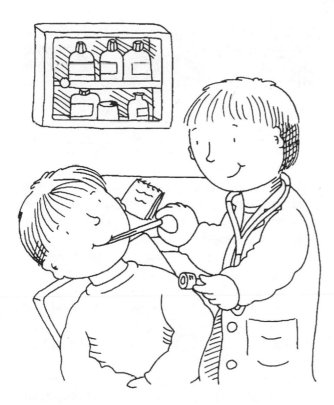

SURGERY TIME

● ●

Objective

PE/Drama — To encourage role-play.

Group size

Six to eight children.

What you need

A toy 'doctor's kit' with stethoscope, thermometer, bandages, cotton wool and so on. A large piece of cardboard, marker pen. The role-play area set up as a health clinic with a table and chair for the doctor, chairs for the patients, rows of chairs in a 'waiting area', and a table and chair for the receptionist. A home-made appointments book and prescription pad, two toy telephones, soft toys or dolls.

Preparation

Make a large sign saying 'Surgery — Open from 9.30 to 12.30'. Take the children for a walk to the nearest doctor's surgery or health centre. Look at the plate giving the doctors' names. Point out the time of opening. If possible, arrange to take the children inside to see the waiting room and reception desk.

What to do

Group the children on the carpet and talk about their visit to the surgery. Ask them to recall the times when they have been to see the doctor. Look at and talk about the doctor's kit.

Tell the children that the role-play area is going to become a doctor's surgery. Explain the layout and special equipment. Choose some children to be the doctor, receptionist and patients. They may like to use soft toys or dolls as patients.

Encourage the children to role-play the suggested activities below:

✧ Making an appointment to see the doctor: the receptionist answers the phone and writes the appointment in the book.

✧ Bringing a child to the surgery: the receptionist looks in the appointment book to check that an appointment has been made, then sends the people to wait for the doctor.

✧ Calling the patient to see the doctor in her room: the parent explains the child's symptoms and the doctor examines the child, explains the treatment and writes a prescription.

Discussion

How does the doctor find out what is wrong with a patient? Think about the things that a doctor does to make people better. Tell the children about home-visits. Talk about the role of the receptionist.

Follow-up activities

✧ Set up a 'medical display' (stethoscope, thermometer, bandages).

✧ Sing the song 'Miss Polly had a dolly who was sick, sick, sick', in *This Little Puffin*, Elizabeth Matterson (Puffin).

THE HAIRDRESSER

Objective

Art – To select various items associated with hairdressing and explore the range of prints that can be made.

Group size

Up to six children.

What you need

Different colours of thick paint, plastic trays, paintbrushes, a selection of different sized and shaped rollers, grips, a comb, a hairbrush, some blunt-ended scissors, a selection of shampoo bottles and caps. Large sheets of coloured paper or card. Aprons for the children.

Preparation

Cut head and shoulder shapes out of the coloured paper or card. Prepare the paints and put different colours into the plastic trays. Ask the children to sort the hairdressing items into trays and place them on the table. Put an apron for each child by each space.

What to do

Ask each child to put on an apron. Show the children the objects on the table and ask if they know what they are. Pick examples of the objects up as they are recognised and discuss how they are used. Talk about going to the hairdresser, and the need for keeping our hair healthy and clean. Tell the children they are going to design their own hairstyles.

Allow each child to choose a card 'head and shoulders'. Talk about the sort of prints that can be made with the objects. Show the children how to put the objects in the paint trays and print onto the paper.

Invite each child to choose different objects to design their hairstyles. When the heads are finished ask the children to name some of the objects they used and describe how they achieved the print. Write a caption to describe the hairstyle and label it with the child's name.

Discussion

As the children handle and talk about the objects, ask them to think about the role of the hairdresser. Encourage the children to observe each other's hair. Who has brown hair? Who has long hair? Whose hair is curly and whose hair is straight? Who goes to the hairdresser's? Who washes our hair? Why do we need to keep our hair clean and healthy?

Follow-up activities

◇ Make paper plate faces and stick on different materials to represent hair (strips of curled paper, string, wool, raffia, ribbon).
◇ Carry out a survey of children's hair colour. Make a simple pictogram.
◇ Read the poem 'Haircut' in the Resources section on page 69.
◇ Set up the role-play corner as a hairdresser's. Make sure that the children are not cutting each other's hair!
◇ Collect different containers for shampoo and use for sorting, counting and capacity.

AT THE BABY CLINIC

Objective

Mathematics — To introduce, or reinforce the children's concept of weight and length.

Group size

Six or eight children.

What you need

The role-play area set up as a baby clinic. Cardboard, a selection of dolls and teddy bears, a balance pan suitable for weighing dolls and teddy bears, cotton reels or counting cubes, straws, A3 size sheets of paper, felt-tipped pens, crayons and colouring paper, uniforms for the 'health visitors'.

Preparation

Make a sign saying 'Baby Clinic' from cardboard. Make a chart from the A3 paper to record the weights of the dolls and bears (see right). If possible take the children, by prior arrangement, to visit the local baby clinic where they will see the health visitor weighing babies. Ask the health visitor to explain how she helps to keep us healthy.

What to do

Set up the 'baby clinic' in the role-play area with two tables for weighing and measuring dolls and teddy bears. Choose two children to be health visitors and others to be 'parents' of a doll or teddy bear. (Make sure that 'Dads' as well as 'Mums' take 'baby' along to the clinic.) Dolls and teddy bears may be brought from home.

Enable each 'baby' to be undressed, weighed (using the cotton reels or cubes) and then measured with the straws.

Help the children to record the 'baby's' weight and length on the A3 size chart.
For example:

Name	Weight	Length
Ellie	25 cotton reels	2 straws
Jack	40 cotton reels	3 and a bit straws
Sophie	19 cotton reels	1 and a bit straws

Ask a parent to bring in a real baby to be weighed and measured.

Discussion

Ask why it is important for real babies to become a little heavier and longer each week, explaining that dolls and teddy bears stay the same. Which is the heaviest 'baby', and which is the longest? Is the heaviest 'baby' the longest 'baby'? What other work does the health visitor do?

Follow-up activities

✧ Draw round dolls and teddy bears and put them in order of size.
✧ Ask the children to find out what their own birth weights and lengths were. These could be brought in and recorded on a chart.

SHOE MIX UP!

Objective

Mathematics – To introduce the concept of a pair and to develop sorting and matching skills.

Group size

Any size.

What you need

A collection of footwear: (adult's and children's) of different sizes, sorts, colours and fastenings, including pairs and single shoes. Large box or basket, card and felt-tipped pen.

Preparation

Mix the collection of footwear up and place in a large box or basket.

What to do

Ask the children to make a circle and sit on the floor. Tip the box or basket of shoes into the middle of the circle so that all the children can see the shoes.

Ask them what they can see in the shoe mix up. Encourage them to use vocabulary to categorise and describe the footwear. Pick a shoe from the pile and ask a child to find the matching one to make a pair. Encourage the children to describe the shoe so that the other one can be found. What colour is it? How does it fasten? What is it made of? Is it a shoe for an adult or a child? When would you wear it?

When the child has found the matching shoe place the pair together and show the children. Take turns so that the other children can sort and match the shoes to find a pair. When the shoes have been put into pairs collect the ones that don't make a pair. Use the card to make two labels saying: ' Pairs of shoes' and 'These shoes do not have pairs'.

Discussion

Explain the role of the children's shoe specialist. What does the shoe specialist do to find the right size of shoe? How does he or she measure our feet? Why do children have to have new shoes? How can we look after our shoes? Who helps us to keep our feet healthy? How can we look after our feet? What special shoes do we wear?

Follow-up activities

✧ Collect pictures of different footwear from magazines and catalogues. Discuss the different types of shoes, what they are used for and how they are fastened.
✧ Challenge the children to design their own shoes, using cardboard shoe templates. Help the children to cut out the shoes, and choose different materials to create their own.
✧ Learn the traditional nursery rhyme 'The old woman who lived in a shoe'.

SUPER SPECS!

Objective

Design and Technology — To look at different designs of spectacles and design a pair.

Group size

Up to six children at a time.

What you need

A selection of children's and adults' spectacles, sunglasses, ski and swimming goggles, safety glasses and 3D glasses. Old magazines, crayons, paints, felt-tipped pens, adhesive, glitter, thick cardboard, brightly coloured card, small gummed paper shapes, scissors.

Preparation

Collect a selection of different spectacles. Cut out pictures of people wearing spectacles from magazines. Draw round a pair of children's sunglasses on thick cardboard to make a template. Use the template to cut pairs of spectacles out of the brightly coloured card, varying the shape. Have enough spectacles to give children a choice of colour and shape. Make an example pair or two to show the children.

What to do

Show the children the collection of spectacles. Ask them to identify the different sorts and compare the sunglasses to the ordinary spectacles, pointing out the lenses. Can they describe what the spectacles are used for? Explain that many people wear special glasses to protect their eyes at work, in the summer or because their eyes can't see as well as they should. Explain that you have to have a special test at the optician's to find out if you need help to see. If a child has spectacles encourage him or her to talk about the eye test.

Show the children the spectacles you have made. Invite the children to select some of the materials and design their own pair.

When the glasses are finished gather all the children together. Encourage each child to show their spectacles, and talk about the materials they have used. Set up a 'super specs' display with the children's designs. Write a caption: 'We designed our own super specs!'.

Discussion

Why do people need to be able to see well? Encourage the children to think about things that would be difficult to do if we could not see very well, for example, reading, driving. Why are the spectacles different? (Colour, shape, size, style, purpose.)

Follow-up activities

✧ Read the story 'Susie's specs' in the Resources section on page 78.
✧ Look at different aids for the blind (Braille, special sticks, guide dogs).
✧ Ask children to identify familiar objects (a teddy, spoon, toy car, crisps) when blindfolded.

OUR HOSPITAL – THE NURSE

Objective

Geography – To understand the role of the hospital nurse.

Group size

Whole group or class for the introduction, groups of six to eight for the activity.

What you need

A photograph of the local hospital, cardboard, a thick felt-tipped pen. The role-play area set up as a hospital with beds, cots and chairs for out-patients. Two 'play' nurses' uniforms, a toy nurse's kit with thermometer, cotton wool, bandages, small notebooks, pencils, plastic spoons, ointment (Vaseline). The co-operation of a nurse prepared to visit, wearing his or her uniform and willing to talk to the children about his or her job.

Preparation

Make a large sign with the cardboard saying 'Hospital'. Gather the whole group or class on the carpet and ask if anyone has been in hospital (either to stay in or as an out-patient). Encourage the children to describe their experiences. Show them a photograph of the local hospital.

What to do

Invite a hospital nurse to come and visit the group to talk about their work in the hospital. Ask the nurse to talk about the tasks he has to do and the clothes that he has to wear.

Allow one group of children at a time into the 'hospital'. Suggest the role-play group can have two nurses, one attending the 'out-patients' and one attending to 'in-patients'. The 'in-patients' can be dolls and teddy bears, and children can act as 'out-patients'.

Discussion

Encourage the children to think of times when people need to go to hospital but don't have to stay in. What kinds of treatment does the nurse give? Why do people have to stay in hospital? What does the nurse do to help people feel better? Who else works in a hospital as well as nurses?

Follow-up activities

✧ Reinforce 'People who keep us healthy' by using the photocopiable activity sheet on page 92.
✧ Make a large collage of a nurse. Display with a caption saying 'A nurse helps us at the hospital'.
✧ Make models of ambulances and hospitals out of junk boxes, LEGO and Sticklebricks.
✧ Plan whole group sessions on 'safety'. For older children you may like to discuss the fact that they should only take medicine when told by a doctor, nurse or parents.

CHAPTER 4
KEEPING US SAFE

Children love to hear about brave people and will often include situations involving the emergency services and rescue operations in their imaginative play. Through the activities in this chapter the children will learn about the people that help to create a safe environment for them to grow up in.

FIRE-FIGHTERS

Objective

Design and Technology — To encourage children to design and make moveable fire-engines from reclaimed materials.

Group size

Various.

What you need

Any 'Fireman Sam' book by Rob Lee (Buzz Books). A quantity of reclaimed materials including different sized cartons, boxes, cylinders, art straws and pipe cleaners. Rubber tubing, beads, dowel rods, cardboard and wooden wheels. Strong adhesive, scissors, thick red, white and black paint.

Preparation

Read the chosen 'Fireman Sam' book to the children. Show them the illustrations from the book. If possible make arrangements with the local fire station for a fire-engine and crew to come to the building or take the children on a visit to a fire station if this can be arranged. The crew will explain their role and show the children how a fire-engine works.

What to do

Group the children on the carpet to talk about the visit of the fire-engine and the crew. Suggest that the children might like to make fire-engines and a fire station.

Choose two children to make the fire station. The rest of the children can be grouped around a pre-prepared table with the reclaimed materials placed in the middle. Explain that the fire-engines should have wheels that move and ladders. Encourage children to suggest materials that might be appropriate and consider how these materials can be joined.

Discussion

How do the fire-engines get inside the fire station? What clothing does a fire-fighter wear? How do fire-fighters know there is a fire? How do fire-fighters travel to a fire? What colour are the fire-engines? How do people know a fire-engine is rushing to a fire? What equipment do fire-fighters have to help put out a fire? Explain that sometimes fire-fighters have to enter a building to rescue people and put out the fire. What do fire-fighters use to help them breathe when they go into a burning smoky building? How are fires extinguished? What do we need to do regularly so that we know what to do in the event of fire?

Follow-up activities

◇ Learn the action poem 'The fireman' in the Resources section on page 70.
◇ Organise a fire drill. Discuss the procedures with the children before and after the fire.
◇ Make a frieze of 'The fire-fighters'. Include buildings, fire-engines, fire-fighters and people.
◇ Sing the song 'Fireman Fred' in the Resources section on page 81.
◇ Make ladders with different numbers of rungs. Write numbers on the rungs to use as number lines.

THE POLICE OFFICER

Objective

Drama – To encourage children to think about and act out various tasks of a police officer.

Group size

Six to ten children.

What you need

Several hats (as worn by policemen and women), a toy steering wheel, building blocks, cardboard, a thick felt-tipped pen, a flip chart or similar. The role-play area set up as a police station with a desk and telephone.

Preparation

Make a large sign saying 'Police Station'. Arrange a visit to the local police station. Take the children to visit, in groups of six to ten. Arrange for someone to explain some of the jobs a police officer does. Emphasise the caring, helpful role of the police.

What to do

Ask the children to think of all the jobs the police officer does to keep us safe. Write these down on the flip chart. Read through the list with the children. Use the following situations for dramas:
✧ The telephone rings at the police station and an emergency call is taken. A man says the traffic lights have broken down at the nearby crossroads. The desk police officer rings the panda car and asks two police officers to travel to the broken lights. One of the officers can direct the traffic.
✧ A man phones the police station to say the burglar alarm is going off in his next door neighbour's house. Two police officers are sent in the panda car to the house. They arrest a burglar who is trying to steal the television set.
✧ A little girl is crying because she is lost, she finds a policewoman in a busy shopping centre. She gives the policewoman her name and address. The policewoman puts a message across the loudspeaker system, explaining to the little girl that she is safe with her until her mummy arrives. The anxious mother collects her child.

Discussion

What tasks do the police carry out? Discuss each scenario with the children. How would the man who phoned about the broken traffic lights explain what had happened? How does a police officer direct the traffic? What would the police officer say to the burglar? How would you feel if you were lost in a big, crowded shop? What would you do?

Follow-up activities

✧ Make large collages of a policeman and woman.
✧ Hold a 'Stranger Danger' day or week. Ask a police officer to come and talk to the children about 'stranger danger'.

ACTIVITIES
36
PEOPLE WHO HELP US

THE AMBULANCE SERVICE

Objective

Design and Technology — To assist children to make moveable ambulances from reclaimed materials and construction apparatus.

Group size

Six or eight children, working in pairs or individually.

What you need

Pictures, posters, leaflets from the local ambulance service (address in Yellow Pages). Various sizes and lengths of dowel rod and plastic tubing cut into short pieces for axles, beads (used as stoppers on axles). A selection of cardboard and wooden wheels. Adhesive, scissors, adhesive tape, paper fasteners. White, black, blue and red paints, felt-tipped pens, paintbrushes, aprons. A variety of boxes, cartons and tubes. A plentiful supply of construction apparatus with lots of sets of wheels. A toy model ambulance.

Preparation

Cover and prepare a table for the model-making. Cut the plastic tubing into small parts, and the dowel into suitable lengths for axles. Place the adhesive, scissors, paper fasteners, beads, dowel, plastic tubing and wheels onto the table. Cover another table with newspaper ready for the children to paint their finished and dried models. Prepare thick white, blue, black and red paints. Place

aprons, paint and brushes on the table. Set up another table with the construction apparatus, boxes, cartons and tubes.

What to do

Gather the children on the carpet and set the scene by asking what happens if there is an accident in the road or if somebody suddenly becomes ill at home or work. Show the children the model ambulance and some of the pictures or posters relating to the ambulance service.

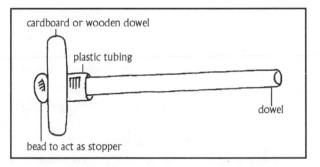

Suggest the children can make ambulances from the boxes and/or the construction apparatus. Encourage the children to think about the construction of their model ambulances. Allow the children to work in pairs or individually. Explain that the wheels need to turn and there must be a space inside for the sick or injured people.

Discussion

How can we make our ambulances move? Who travels inside the ambulance? How do people get into the ambulances? What are the special beds called for carrying injured or sick people into the ambulance? What equipment is needed inside the ambulance? Describe the journey that the ambulance makes to the hospital: will it travel fast or slow, quietly or noisily? What should other road users do when they see or hear an ambulance on the road?

Follow-up activities

✧ Encourage the children to think up their own ambulance stories.
✧ Find information books about the ambulance service. Investigate other services such as St. John's and Red Cross.
✧ Collect toy cars, ambulances, police cars and play people. Make a road scene so that children can carry out role-play activities.

ROAD SAFETY

Objective

English – To encourage children to develop listening and thinking skills.

Group size

A whole class or group. Some parts of the activity will require the support of other adults.

What you need

The services of the local road safety officer (address available from the local police station), a mock pedestrian crossing (borrowed from the road safety department or made from a large roll of black paper painted with white stripes), a set of mock traffic lights (borrowed from the road safety department or made from large boxes and painted in the appropriate colours), a mock red and green 'walking figure' made from boxes. An audio cassette of traffic sounds.

Preparation

Either organise the loan of the pedestrian crossing and traffic lights from the road safety department or make the models. Record traffic sounds. Invite the road safety officer to speak to the children.

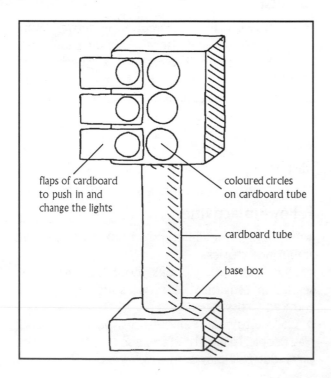

flaps of cardboard to push in and change the lights

coloured circles on cardboard tube

cardboard tube

base box

What to do

Discuss the road safety officer's visit with the whole class or group. Explain that all children should be taught to cross the road safely but emphasise that they must always cross the road with an adult.

Take the children into the hall or any large space and place them in a large circle. Set up the pedestrian crossing.

Explain to the children that they are going to practise crossing a busy road. Use one child to help and demonstrate what we must do to cross safely. Go through the following drill:

✧ Find a safe place to cross (a pedestrian crossing);
✧ Press the crossing button and wait;
✧ Wait for the traffic lights to turn red to stop the traffic;
✧ Look for the 'walking person' to turn from red to green;
✧ Look right, look left, look right again and if all is safe, walk quickly across the road.

Make sure all the children perform this drill. Discuss important points as they do this. Ask another adult to play the traffic sounds tape. Integrate the traffic sounds in a way that will encourage the children to listen carefully while carrying out the activity. As the lights become red the traffic noises should stop. Start the traffic noises again when the lights change back to green.

Discussion

Where is the safest place to cross a busy road? What do you do first when you reach the pedestrian crossing? How can you tell when it is safe to cross? Who should always be with you when you cross the road? Why is it dangerous to run across the road? What would you do if your ball rolled into the road? Ask the children to suggest some safe places to play.

Follow-up activities

✧ Organise a road safety week. Invite the road safety officer, lollipop person and parents to take part. See page 64 for an idea for an assembly.
✧ Teach the children the following song (to the tune of 'Here we go round the mulberry bush'):

This is the way we cross the road, cross the road, cross the road,

This is the way we cross the road, keeping the safety rules.

THE BREAKDOWN PEOPLE

Objective

PE – To experience different ways of moving and to develop a sequence of moves.

Group size

Any size.

What you need

A large space, a tambourine.

What to do

As a warm-up activity ask the children to move around the room, encouraging them to use various ways of travelling, using different body parts and by varying the speed.

Invite the children to think of a way of moving to show a car travelling along the road. Use the tambourine in different ways to represent the movements. Bang the tambourine to signal starting and stopping. Shake the tambourine gradually to indicate movements getting slower and slower. Encourage them to listen to the sound of the tambourine to help them decide on the speed and to tell them when to stop and start. Introduce the idea of waiting, then travelling again around the room without touching anyone.

Explain to the children that their car has broken down. In pairs they can mime some busy movements as they try to mend each other's cars. As you shake the tambourine the car gradually begins to work again and the children can make their way 'home'.

Discussion

What happens if the car breaks down? Who do we call to help us make the car go again? Talk to the children about breakdown services and the way they help people when their cars have broken down. Have the children ever seen a car being towed? Use the movement session to explore vocabulary associated with speed.

Follow-up activities

◇ Make a break-down lorry using construction apparatus or reclaimed materials.
◇ Make a large car out of boxes for the children to play in. Include seats and a steering wheel.
◇ Discuss the emergency telephones on the motorway and their importance to road users.
◇ Collect some equipment that might be found in a car in case of a breakdown (hazard warning triangle, torch, AA/RAC or National Breakdown cards).

THE SAFETY OFFICER

Objective

Science – To understand that toys have to pass safety tests.

Group size

Up to four children.

What you need

A collection of different toys that children are familiar with from home (soft toys, toys with small parts, a boxed toy with the recommended age written on the package, toys for a baby, toddler and older child), a large piece of sugar paper, felt-tipped pens, home-made badges, two labels (saying 'safe' and 'unsafe').

Preparation

Arrange the collection on a table. Make badges saying, 'Safety Officer'. Write a caption on the large sheet of paper 'Safety Report'. Divide the paper into two columns and write: 'Name of toy', and 'Safety report'. Draw sections across the paper for each toy that is to be scrutinised. Make the two lables saying 'safe' and 'unsafe'.

What to do

Gather the children round a table. Show the children the collection of objects to be inspected. Talk about the need to have toys that are safe for children to use. All toys should pass a test to make sure that they are safe for young children to play with. Explain the role of the safety officer. Give the children the home-made badges and tell them that they are going to be safety officers.

Encourage the children to think about what might be safe and not safe on toys (eyes on soft toys, small parts on vehicles, tops on pens, paint on toys). Point out the recommended age on the package.

Look at the selected objects carefully and encourage the children to identify things that are safe and unsafe. Put the toys into two groups with the appropriate 'safe' and 'unsafe' labels. On the 'Safety Report' sheet write down the name of the toy and whether it is safe or unsafe, noting any unsafe details. Display the objects with the 'Safety Report' for the children to examine.

Discussion

What do we need to look for? (Loose eyes on soft toys, small parts that can be taken off.) Would it be safe for babies/toddlers/older children? Why do we look on packages when we are buying toys? Why does it give a recommended age on toys? How can we make sure children have safe toys to play with?

Follow-up activities

✧ Ask the children to bring in safe toys to add to the display.
✧ Encourage the children to design safety posters by drawing pictures of safe and unsafe toys.

MOUNTAIN RESCUE

Objective

RE – To develop an awareness of people who use their special skills and expertise in helping others.

Group size

Up to six children.

What you need

Picture or posters of hills, mountains and mountain rescue teams, large sheets of sugar paper, felt-tipped pens, crayons, information books about mountain rescue.

Preparation

Collect information on mountain rescue teams. Use the large pieces of sugar paper to make zigzag books for each child in the group. Write 'Mountain rescue' and the child's name on the front page.

What to do

Gather the children together and show them pictures or posters of the hills or mountains. Explain that people like to walk and climb the hills and mountains in their leisure time. Emphasise that usually it is safe as long as people take safety precautions (take proper equipment, use maps, take notice of the weather forecast and so on).

Explain that sometimes people need help (accidents happen, the weather gets bad, people get lost) and the mountain rescue people are called out to help. Show them the pictures of and books on mountain rescue.

Present the children with the following scenario:

> Doris and Maurice decide to spend a day out walking in the hills. They pack their rucksack, put on waterproof clothes and walking boots. They plan where to go on the map and tell their friends that they will be back in time for tea.
>
> After they have walked for a while the weather turns stormy. It starts to rain and they feel cold. A mist comes down and they can't see the way. Soon they are lost. They decide to sit down and wait for help.
>
> When they don't arrive back for tea their friends are worried and they call the mountain rescue team for help. The mountain rescue team search the area and bring them back safely.

Ask the children to draw pictures and, if they can, write the story of the rescue in the right order in their zigzag books.

Discussion

Why do people need to listen to the weather forecast? What equipment would be useful to carry? Why do you need to tell people where you are going? What is special about the mountain rescue team?

Follow-up activities

✧ Look at special equipment that might be carried by walkers and climbers (maps, compass, first aid box).
✧ Investigate how people send messages for help.

A BRAVE RESCUE

Objective

History – To learn about a famous person from the past.

Group size

Up to six children.

What you need

The Lighthouse Keeper's Catastrophe by Ronda and David Armitage (Picture Puffin). A simplified version of the story of Grace Darling. Sheets of blue paper, felt-tipped pens, crayons, pencils, large sheets of coloured sugar paper, thin sheet of card.

Preparation

Read *The Lighthouse Keeper's Catastrophe* to the children, which is about the problems a lighthouse keeper has carrying out his job when he loses the keys to his lighthouse. Discuss the role of the lighthouse keeper and emphasise how he or she helps keep people safe. Make a book for the children's stories. Cut out a large rowing boat and stick it on the front card cover. Write the title 'A brave rescue – the story of Grace Darling'.

What to do

Remind the children of the story of *The Lighthouse Keeper's Catastrophe* and relate this to the story of Grace Darling (1815 – 42).

Tell the children about Grace Darling, explain that Grace's father was the keeper of a lighthouse. During a storm a steamship was wrecked on rocks. As it was too rough to launch the lifeboat Grace and her father bravely decided to row to rescue the crew. Suggest the children draw and write about Grace and her father rescuing the sailors.

Show the home-made book 'A brave rescue - the story of Grace Darling' to the children. Invite a few of the children to complete the boat to include Grace, her father and the rescued sailors. Fill the book with the children's drawings and stories. Display the completed book in the library area.

Discussion

Ask the children if they think Grace was brave. Why was Grace brave? What had happened to the steamship? How did Grace help her father? What did Mr Darling do to help people keep away from the rocks? Explain that the sea can be fun but also dangerous. Why do we need lifeboats at the seaside?

Follow-up activities

✧ Collect posters and pictures of lighthouses and lifeboats to display.
✧ Listen to pieces of music connected with the sea (such as 'Fingal's Cave' by Mendelssohn).
✧ Introduce a collection of plastic boats into the water tray and encourage the children to load objects until they sink.

CHAPTER 5
BRINGING OUR FOOD

Children have a natural enthusiasm for food and enjoy playing 'shops'. The activities in this chapter will broaden their knowledge of the people that work to bring their food to them, where their food comes from and how it reaches them.

LORRY DRIVER

Objective

PE/Drama – To develop imaginative play and the use of appropriate language for a situation.

Group size

Any size.

What you need

A collection of cardboard boxes (representing the packed food transported in the lorries), large plastic or wooden building bricks, large and small chairs, small tables, a toy steering wheel, cut out cardboard circles or PE hoops (for wheels), a snow sweeper (to make a snow plough), flask and sandwich box.

Preparation

Tell the story of Jackie and Albert's busy day:

The workers in the food factory pack the lorry with big boxes to be transported to a supermarket in the next town. The boxes are counted as they are packed. Jackie and Albert set off on their journey, taking turns to drive. Snow starts to fall. They decide to stop in a lay-by. They eat their sandwiches and drink their coffee, and talk about what they are going to do. A police car comes along and the police tell Jackie and Albert that the snow plough will come to help them. The snow plough arrives. Jackie, Albert and the police cheer. The snow plough clears the road ahead. Jackie and Albert arrive at the supermarket. The workers come out to cheer. They hadn't expected to see the lorry. The lorry is unloaded. Jackie, Albert, the police and the workers have a drink in the canteen.

What to do

Invite the children to build Jackie and Albert's lorry, the police car and the snow plough. Provide them with the building bricks, chairs, tables and other materials.

Help the children to act out the story, using the simple sentences to structure their imaginative role-play. Ask the children for suggestions to develop the story.

Discussion

What foods were in the boxes? Why were there two lorry drivers? Why do they need to rest? Why did Jackie and Albert have sandwiches and a flask? What was in the flask? Who came to the rescue? Why did the snow plough go first? Were the workers pleased to see the lorry arrive?

Follow-up activities

◇ Make lorries using reclaimed materials. Cut food pictures from magazines to stick on the lorries.
◇ Make a collage showing the episodes of the story.
◇ Collect a selection of boxes and objects of different sizes and shape. Discover what fits into the boxes.

THE SHOPKEEPER

Objective

History — To help children understand the differences between the role of a present day shopkeeper and that of a shopkeeper in the past.

Group size

Six or eight children at a time.

What you need

A willing grandparent or adult born in the 1930's or 1940's. Small tables, shelves (book shelves can be emptied temporarily and used for this purpose). Balance pans, a toy till, play dough in a variety of colours, paper bags and squares of kitchen paper for wrapping up goods, coins, labels, small pieces of card, felt-tipped pens, paper, overalls, photographs or pictures of shops forty years ago.

Preparation

Take the children on a visit to the nearest large supermarket. Explain that most things we need to eat can now be bought in one shop. Point out that people walk around the shop with a trolley, collecting the things they need. Most things are in packets, tins and plastic containers. Customers pay at the checkout.

Invite an older person to talk to the children about shops they remember when they were children, pointing out the differences between then and now.

What to do

Show the children the photographs and pictures of old fashioned shops. Suggest that the children should make an 'old fashioned' shop. Ask for ideas about the kind of shop it could be — a grocer's, a greengrocer's, a baker's or a sweet shop.

Help the children to set up the shop by placing small tables and shelves in appropriate positions. Ask the children to suggest a name for the shop and write it on a long strip of card and fix it on to the counter. Help the children to make goods for the shop with the play dough and write the price labels.

Choose two children to be the shopkeepers, one as 'errand boy/girl', and the others as customers. The customers could make 'shopping lists' with adult help. The shopkeepers could weigh and wrap various goods. The errand boy/delivery person could take the goods to other children in the group.

Discussion

Think of all the differences between supermarket shopping today and shopping when the children's grandparents were young. How would the goods be weighed? How would the shopkeeper wrap the goods? What happened if the customer bought a large number of goods?

Follow-up activities

✧ Extend this activity by giving the children the photocopiable sheet on page 93. Talk about the different people and food shown on the sheet. Ask the children to draw a line to match the correct food to each person.

✧ Make a frieze of the different kinds of shops we see today.

✧ Do a high street or local shopping centre walk to see how many shops are butchers, bakers, newsagents or supermarkets.

✧ Read the poem 'Supermarket Sam' in the Resources section on page 69.

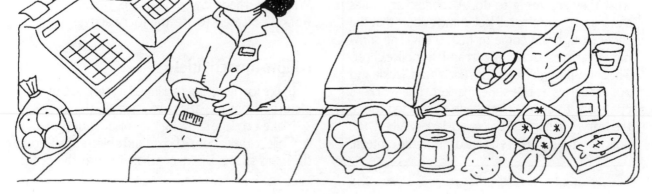

FOOD FACTORY

Objective

Design and Technology — To assist children to make and package foods.

Group size

Between six and eight children.

What you need

A mixing bowl, flour, fat and water to make a simple dough for biscuits, an oven, different shaped pastry cutters, plain envelopes, felt-tipped pens, clear plastic film, a stapler, adhesive tape, shoeboxes, overalls, paper-clips. Photographs and pictures of food factories.

Preparation

Ask children how they think food such as biscuits, cakes, yoghurts and tins of baked beans arrive in the supermarket. Explain that many foods are made in factories. Show the photographs and pictures of food factories.

What to do

Ask the children to put on the overalls. Explain that they are going to set up a food factory.

Choose two children to make biscuits while others decorate and label the plain envelopes for the packaging for the biscuits. After the biscuits have been cooked, ask two children to pack the biscuits, firstly in cling film and then into the packets. Finally, staple the packets or seal them with adhesive tape. Then show the children how to pack them into the shoeboxes.

Discussion

Ask the children how they think a biscuit factory works. Do all the people make biscuits? What other jobs are there to do? Who designs the packages? Why is it important to have clean hands, overalls and a cap when handling food? How can we make sure the biscuits stay fresh? How will the boxes be delivered to the shops?

Follow-up activities

✧ Collect food labels and different types of packaging and make them into a montage.
✧ Draw and paint pictures of people working in food factories.
✧ Write a group story about people in food factories. Encourage the children to suggest ideas and ask an adult to act as scribe.

DELIVERING MILK

Objective

Mathematics – To learn about liquid capacity.

Group size

Six to ten children.

What you need

Plastic bottles of different sizes, a measuring jug, a large jug of milk, pictures of milk deliverers and milk floats, and/or a book showing pictures of someone delivering milk.

Preparation

If possible, arrange to observe a local milk deliverer at work, alternatively show the children some pictures of someone delivering the milk.

What to do

Talk to the children about the things that a milk deliverer does such as collecting empty bottles and delivering extra pints.

Show children the different sized bottles. Pour some milk into the measuring jug. Ask the children to estimate whether or not this quantity would fill the large bottle. Try it and see. Would it fill the small bottle? Would there be too much? Pour the milk back into the jug. Ask the children to estimate how many small bottles it would take to fill the large bottle. Pour the milk into the small bottle and use this to fill the large bottle.

Discussion

Encourage the children to recall the work of the milk deliverer. How is the milk transported? Where are the bottles kept? How many bottles fit into a crate? How does the milk deliverer know how many bottles to leave at each house? What other things are made of milk? (Milkshakes, custard, rice pudding, butter.)

Follow-up activities

✧ Make custard or blancmange with the children and let them taste it.
✧ Find out where milk comes from. What happens to it before it reaches us?
✧ Find out how milk was delivered years ago, before the days of special milk bottles and electric floats.
✧ Investigate the different types of milk that are available (semi-skimmed, skimmed, full milk, sterilised, gold top, Soya). Organise a 'tasting' and ask the children which is their favourite. Make a graph to show the results of the tasting. (Be aware of any allergies.)

THE BAKER

Objective

Music – To enable children to sing a song from memory and combine actions.

Group size

Any size.

What you need

A selection of bread: rolls (plain and with poppy and sunflower seeds on the top), buns, sliced loaf, cottage loaf, French stick and cobs. A toy till, real or play money, purses, shopping bags, an overall and a baker's hat, small table, table-cloth, the poem 'Bakery rhyme' from the Resources section on page 73, traditional rhyme 'Five currant buns'.

Preparation

Put a cloth on a small table. Place the selection of bread on the cloth. Collect the toy till, money, purses, shopping bags, overall and baker's hat and keep to one side. Put a selection of small coins into the purses. Put some coins into the till.

What to do

Gather the whole group together. Read the poem 'Bakery rhyme'. Show the children the different types of bread.

Change the words of the rhyme 'Five currant buns...' to:

'Five lovely loaves in the baker's shop, golden brown – some with seeds on the top, along came... with her/his money one day, bought a lovely loaf (French stick etc.) and took it away.'

Sing the rhyme and add the actions, choosing a child to be the baker and children to be the customers (give these children the purses). The customers choose some bread, and pay for it. The baker takes the money, giving change if required. The customer waves goodbye and sits down.

Discussion

What sorts of bread do you see in a baker's shop? Where else can you buy bread? Why is bread sliced and put into wrappers? What other things might you find in a baker's shop? If the children have a packed lunch ask what sort of bread they usually have.

Follow-up activities

✧ Make bread with the children.
✧ Carry out a survey to discover which bread the birds like best (always soak the bread in milk or water first).
✧ Read the Bible story of 'The feeding of the five thousand'.
✧ Make sandwiches using different fillings. Cut the bread into different shapes.
✧ Arrange a visit to a baker's shop to see what other things the baker sells.
✧ Make the role-play corner into a baker's shop. Make cakes and bread from salt dough.
✧ Sing 'Pat-a-cake, pat-a-cake baker's man'.

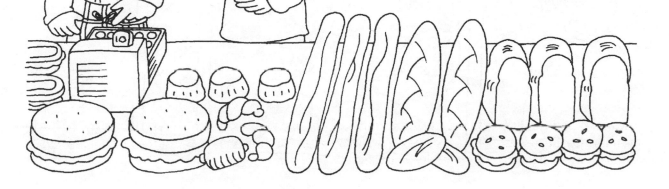

GONE FISHING!

Objective

Art – To involve children in making a game using a variety of resources and materials.

Group size

Up to eight children.

What you need

A large cardboard box, four overhead transparencies/pieces of strong polythene/clear plastic film, small pieces of stiff card, white card, felt-tipped pens, crayons, a selection of wrapping paper, tissue paper, small pieces of material, adhesive, scissors, paper-clips, garden sticks, string, small round magnets, newspaper, thick blue and green paint, paintbrushes, aprons.

Preparation

Cut a section out of the sides of the cardboard box leaving a frame. Take the overhead transparencies, polythene or plastic film and stick to the inside of the box to make 'windows' in the sides. Cut fish templates out of stiff card. Cut a selection of different sized pieces out of the white card. Cut the string into lengths of about 45 centimetres. Cover two tables with newspaper: on one, place the large box, paints, brushes and aprons; on the other table arrange the rest of the resources. Make a couple of fish using the different materials. Attach the paper-clip to the mouth of the fish. Fasten a length of string to the top of the garden stick. Attach the magnet to the other end.

What to do

Show the children the box, fish and fishing rods. Tell them they are going to make a fishing game. Show the children how the fish have been made and ask them to identify the materials that were used.

Invite two children to paint the inside of the box to represent the water and the others in the group to make the fish using the materials.

When the children have made the fish, hand them each a rod and show them how to catch the fish with their magnets. Can the children invent some simple rules or variations to the game?

Discussion

Discuss the role of fishermen with the children; how they work at sea to catch the fish that we eat. Where are fish found? (In the sea, lakes, rivers and so on.) How do people catch fish? What do fish look like? How can we make our fish different?

Follow-up activities

✧ Learn and dramatise the rhyme 'One, two, three, four, five …once I caught a fish alive'.
✧ Collect pictures of different fish. Encourage the children to observe the different features. Find out if the fish live in sea water or fresh water.
✧ Explain what happens before fish arrive at the shops for us to buy.

THE MARKET STALL HOLDER

Objective

Geography – To develop children's awareness of their local environment and the importance of the wider world.

Group size

Up to six children.

What you need

Pictures, posters and books showing markets in different parts of the world. A selection of fruit from different countries (orange, lemon, apple, banana, melon, pear, pineapple, mango), paints, paintbrushes, felt-tipped pens, scissors, large sheets of white paper, sheets of paper in two bright colours, a piece of expanding garden trellis, long pieces of thick cardboard, a staple gun, staples, adhesive tape, green 'grass' material, pieces of card, aprons.

Preparation

Collect market pictures and posters. Make a display area with wall and cupboard/table top space. Use the garden trellis to form a market stall canopy. Attach the extended trellis along the display area. Secure with staples and long pieces of thick cardboard. Cover with strips of the brightly coloured paper. Fix the green fabric or 'grass' to hang from the wall onto the flat surface. Place brushes, felt-tipped pens and prepared paints on covered tables. Cut out head and shoulders from card for the stallholders. Display a variety of fruit.

What to do

Ask the children if they have visited a market. Show the children the market display area and the different fruit. Invite them to make a fruit stall.

Invite the children to paint a fruit for the market stall. Choose a couple of children to paint the stallholders. When the paintings are dry, ask the children to add finer details using felt-tipped pens (spots on the bananas, seeds on the strawberries, stalks on the apples, features on stallholders). Add some real fruit to the table top and make price labels with the children.

Discussion

Ask the children if they have visited a market. What stalls did they see? Who sells the goods on the stalls? Explain that stallholders get up very early to buy fruit from the wholesale market for their customers. How is the fruit arranged? How do customers know the price of the fruit?

Follow-up activities

◇ Organise a visit to the local market.
◇ Have a tasting session to try different fruits.
◇ Buy a selection of exotic fruits and find out which country it comes from.

THE FARMER

Objective

English – To listen to a poem and respond by writing a story.

Group size

Up to six children.

What you need

The 'Farmer' poem (in the Resources section on page 71), a large sheet of white paper, a table, large felt-tipped pen, medium and small felt-tipped pens, sheets of brightly coloured paper, pencils, wax crayons, pictures and books showing farm animals and buildings.

Preparation

Write a label at the top of the large sheet of white paper saying: 'The farmer's day.' Prepare a table for the story writing and drawing activity. Place the writing/drawing materials and paper on the table.

What to do

Read the 'Farmer' poem aloud and discuss it with the children.

Place the large sheet of paper where all the children can see it easily.

Encourage the children to identify all the jobs that the farmer has to do in the day. As the children say the jobs list them simply on the large sheet of paper.

Ask each child to choose an activity from the list (or think up a new one) and make up a short sentence for a group story. Ask them to draw and colour a picture to illustrate their sentence. Older children could write out their sentence but younger children may need the support of an adult. Allow the children to refer to the pictures and books of farm animals for details.

When the sentences have been completed make them into a large book. Complete the cover by writing the caption: 'The farmer's day', written by ... (add the children's names) and ask some of the children to illustrate the front cover. Place the book on display or in a book area and encourage the children to read their own book.

Discussion

Talk about the farmer in the poem. Is the farmer male or female? (Ensure that the children are aware that farmers can be men or women.) When does the farmer start work? How do we know it is early in the morning? Explain that male, female and baby animals can have different names (ram, ewe, lamb).

Follow-up activities

✧ Provide a farm set for the children to play with. Make sure there is a female farmer too.
✧ Learn what happens to milk after it leaves the farm until it is delivered by the milk deliverer.
✧ Learn the game: 'The Farmer's in the den'.
✧ Arrange a visit to a farm or farm park.
✧ Learn the names of the male, female and baby animals found on a farm.

CHAPTER 6
CARING FOR THE ENVIRONMENT

As children begin to become more aware of the world they live in it is important for them to appreciate the ways in which people can help to keep their environment clean and attractive. In this chapter we will look at recycling rubbish, painting, decorating and gardening among other things.

A LOAD OF RUBBISH!

Objective
Mathematics – To develop children's understanding of data handling.

Group size
Any size.

What you need
A large sheet of white paper, felt-tipped pens, a rubbish bin, pencils, small pieces of card, glue stick, some disposable rubber gloves, a large piece of polythene, a selection of rubbish (plastic bottle, cardboard tube, plastic cutlery, paper towel, drink can, sweet paper, crisp bag, an apple core, some old clothes).

Preparation
Put the rubbish into a large litter bin. Make a chart with four columns on the large sheet of paper. Write the headings: 'Rubbish'; 'It's made of'; 'Is it recyclable?'; 'In the bin?' at the top of each column. Write: 'yes'; 'no'; 'paper'; 'metal'; 'plastic'; 'cloth'; 'food' on the small pieces of card. Spread the large piece of sheeting on the floor.

What to do
It is important to be aware of health and safety for this activity. Children should not be allowed to touch, eat or smell the rubbish.

Ask the children to sit round the plastic sheet. Place the litter bin and gloves in the middle. Ask the children what they think is in the litter bin. Put on the plastic gloves. Tip out the rubbish. How many things can they name? Invite the children to say what the items are made of. Ask the children what happens to their rubbish at home.

Suggest that some rubbish can be used again, some can be recycled and some has to be taken away by the refuse collectors. Show the children the chart and explain the headings. Pick up an item and demonstrate how to fill in the chart: draw the object on one side and select the ready-made cards to stick into the appropriate columns. Invite the children to complete the chart using the remaining rubbish. Encourage the children to look at the information on the chart. Count how many things were made of plastic. How many items can be taken to the recycling centre?

Discussion
Why do we put rubbish in special containers? How many kinds of rubbish are in the bin? What would happen if we put our rubbish everywhere? What do we need to do to take care of our world? How can we help the refuse collectors? Why do we need to sort the rubbish? What happens to rubbish when it is taken away?

Follow-up activities
✧ Sing the action song 'The wheelie bin song' in the Resources section on page 83.
✧ Take the children to the nearest recycling centre to see how rubbish is sorted into the large containers.
✧ Make some anti-litter posters to display around the building.
✧ Find out when the refuse collectors come to the school/area and take the children to watch them empty the rubbish.

THE GARDEN CENTRE

Objective

English – To name and describe gardening objects. To make labels for a role-play activity.

Group size

Up to six children.

What you need

A large cardboard box, a selection of gardening objects that could be found in a garden centre (trowel, fork, children's hoe and rake, gardening gloves, seed packets, plant pots, seed trays, bulbs, silk flowers, watering can, wheelbarrow). Cupboard or table top, piece of expanding garden trellis, pieces of card, felt-tipped pens, coloured cardboard, wax crayons, large sheets of coloured paper, a play till, toy money, old till receipts.

Preparation

Set up the table or cupboard top. Expand the garden trellis and attach to the back of the cupboard or table top. Cut up the card into suitable sizes for labels and price tags. Place the gardening items into the cardboard box.

What to do

Invite children to help sort out the contents of the cardboard box. Suggest that the objects be sorted into sets of things. Encourage the children to suggest ways of sorting, for example, plant pots, seed packets, garden tools.

When they have sorted them into sets ask the children to describe what the objects are. Encourage them to explain how the things are used and where they can be found.

Challenge the children to make a 'Garden centre' for a role-play activity. Invite them to make their own labels and price tags. Suggest they make posters to advertise their garden centre. Allow them to decide where and how to display their gardening items. Give the children time to play together in the 'Garden centre'.

Discussion

When children are sorting the gardening objects, encourage them to describe the textures, colours and materials. What are the tools used for? How do you know what seeds are in the packets? How can we make our gardens lovely? What vegetables can we grow? What else can you buy at the garden centre? How do people know the prices?

Follow-up activities

✧ Give the children the photocopiable sheet on page 94 and ask them to draw the lines to complete the missing puzzle pieces. Ask them to name the object shown.
✧ Grow different seeds (cress, sunflower, beans and peas). Measure their growth and keep a record.
✧ Use the plant pots, watering cans and containers for capacity activities.
✧ Design seed packets with instructions for growing and an illustration of the flower or vegetable.
✧ If possible arrange for the children to have a piece of garden of their own. Give children different tasks to help maintain the garden.
✧ Organise a visit to a garden or park to look at the flowers and shrubs.
✧ Sing the rhyme 'Mary, Mary, quite contrary'.
✧ Create a 'garden centre' display using the ideas on page 60.

PAINTERS AND DECORATORS

Objective

PE/Drama – To use movement to represent the work of painters and decorators.

Group size

Whole class.

What you need

Large space, paint tin, paint roller, paint tray, paintbrush, colour cards of paints.

What to do

Ask the children if they have seen painters and decorators at work. Have they seen their parents decorating their home? Show the children the objects that are used for decorating. Explain how they are used.

Take the children into the hall or large room. Ask them to lie on the floor with closed eyes and imagine that there is a big wall in front of them. Suggest that the children are going to mime how they would decorate the wall in their favourite colour.

Ask the children to stand up very slowly, pretend to pick up the paint roller and dip it into the paint tray. Climb up the ladder, and paint the wall. Encourage the children to decorate all parts of the wall. Make sure they use a variety of arm and body movements such as stretching and bending. Stand back and admire your work. How would you paint the rest of the room? Suggest that the children paint the door. Choose a different colour and different tools.

Discussion

What do you need if you are going to decorate a room? How could you choose the colours? Why do we decorate our rooms? How would you reach the higher parts of the walls or the ceiling? Which would you use to paint a large wall – the brush or the roller? How do painters and decorators make sure there isn't too much paint on the brush?

Follow-up activities

✧ Invite the children to be interior designers. Make and decorate the inside of a cardboard box to make a room. Use different materials to make some home-made or doll's house furniture to use.
✧ Carry out a survey of children's favourite colours. Put the information onto a graph and use for number work.
✧ Talk about colour moods (red for anger, blue for calm) and how colours are used in the environment (traffic and information signs).
✧ Make a collection of different painting and decorating tools. Try the tools and experiment with different techniques.

THE PARK RANGERS

Objective

Geography — To develop children's awareness of the need to care for the countryside.

Group size

Whole class.

What you need

A sheet of white paper / large white board, water-based pen, copy of the poem 'We must protect the countryside' from the Resources section, page 73.

Preparation

Write a large caption saying, 'Protecting our countryside' at the top of the board or paper. Print out a copy of the poem using large, bold type so that the children can read it clearly.

What to do

Read the poem to the children. Explain to them that many years ago there were a lot more areas of countryside all over Britain.

Encourage them to think about the area around them and ask them to suggest what has happened to many of the fields and forests (building of towns, motorways, shopping malls). Tell the children that large areas of the country have been kept as parks and protected nature reserves that need to be looked after. Explain the role of the park ranger / warden. Encourage children to think about all the jobs that a park ranger has to do. Write their suggestions on the white board or large sheet of paper. Re-read the poem and suggest that the children join in. Display a copy of the poem for the children to read.

Discussion

Why should we look after the countryside? What happens if people drop litter? (Dangerous to animals and people, becomes untidy and unhealthy, spoils the countryside). Can we pick the wild flowers? What would happen if everybody picked flowers? What does the park ranger do? Why do people go to the parks? (To walk, look at the scenery, have picnics, ride bikes). How can we help park rangers to do their job?

Follow-up activities

✧ Make a large model of a country park. Include grass, routes, seats, a play area, water area, car parks.
✧ Read and discuss the country code.
✧ Make posters to show how we can all help care for the countryside.
✧ Visit a local park. Organise a picnic and include 'clearing up' as an activity.
✧ Contact the local wildlife groups in the area. Invite a speaker to talk to children and parents.

ARTISTS

∗ ∘ ∗ ∘ ∗ ∘ ∗ ∘ ∗ ∘ ∗ ∘ ∗ ∘ ∗ ∘ ∗ ∘ ∗ ∘ ∗ ∘ ∗

Objective

Art – To develop children's awareness of artists as 'storytellers'.

Group size

Six to eight children.

What you need

An oil painting, water-colour painting, sugar paper, brushes, powder paints, water pots, adhesive, overalls or aprons, easels or tables, newspaper.

Preparation

Make up the paints. Use adhesive to thicken the powder paint. Cover the tables with newspaper. Arrange brushes, paint pots, water pots, paper and aprons on the tables or near easels. Display oil and water-colour paintings on easels.

What to do

Gather the children together on the carpet. Draw their attention to the oil and water-colour paintings. Encourage them to talk about some of the differences. Suggest to the children that all pictures tell a story.

Share a picture book with the children and draw their attention to the way that the artist tells the story through pictures. The artist's drawings help us to understand the story and they make it fun to share.

Tell the children a traditional story that they know well such as 'Little Red Riding Hood' or 'Jack and the Beanstalk'. Ask them to recall the main parts of the story and suggest that they might like to tell the story through pictures like an artist. Allow each child the opportunity to choose a section of the story to paint.

Discussion

What do we call the people who create pictures? How do they help us learn about the world? Allow the children to touch the paintings – how do they feel? Has the artist used light or dark colours? What is the story in the painting?

Follow-up activities

✧ Arrange for the children to visit a professional artist at work or organise an art in residence week.
✧ Set up an area of your setting as an art gallery for children and adults to display their work. Invite other children and adults to visit the exhibition.
✧ Talk about the work of other artists in other media (sculpture, design, textiles, ceramics, photography).
✧ Look at paintings in the National Gallery using the CD-ROM 'Art Gallery' (Microsoft) and information books.
✧ Visit a local art exhibition (library, museum). If possible, arrange for the children to display their work in a public place (library, supermarket, theatre).

WINDOW CLEANERS

Objective

Science — To compare everyday materials for a particular purpose.

Group size

Up to four children.

What you need

A large window, poster paint, four empty plastic spray containers, mild-washing up liquid, lemon juice, water, vinegar, sheets of newspaper, window cleaning fluid (spray type), cleaning cloths, aprons, labels, felt-tipped pens.

Preparation

Choose a suitable area of window within comfortable range of children's reach. Use the poster paint to divide the window into equal areas. Make the following mixtures: vinegar with water, add lemon juice to water, and add a few drops of washing-up liquid to water. Fill the containers with the different mixes and leave one with just water in. Screw up the newspaper. Make labels to stick onto the containers to show the contents. (Be aware of any allergies to these products).

What to do

Gather the children around the window. Ask them to consider why we need to have clean windows.

Invite the children to clean the window with the different mixtures and screwed up newspaper to see which gives the best results. Before they try them out ask the children to guess which will have the best result. Make sure each child wears an overall. Allocate the different cleaning materials to each child and allow them to clean their section of window.

When the task is completed bring the children back together to look at the finished effect. Decide which section of the window is the cleanest. Was this the one that the children guessed? Write a label describing the experiment and display it with the cleaning materials.

Discussion

Who cleans the windows in your home? What equipment do window cleaners need to carry out their job? How do they reach upstairs windows? How do window cleaners clean tall buildings? What do you need to dry windows? Do you need to clean both sides of the window?

Follow-up activities

✧ Organise a walk to look at different geometrical shapes of windows.
✧ Carry out a survey of different cleaning materials used at home to clean windows.
✧ Make some window frames from cardboard. Ask the children to paint what they can see from some windows. Use the 'windows' to frame their paintings.
✧ Investigate stained glass windows in churches and houses. Make examples using coloured tissue.

NATURE WATCH

Objective

RE – To develop children's awareness of the world around them and to encourage them to care for living creatures.

Group size

Up to six children.

What you need

Access to an outside grassy area with trees and shrubs. Two or three large stones, some old logs or pieces of wood, a large piece of white paper, clipboards, pieces of paper, pencils, crayons, information and story books and pictures of common minibeasts (ladybird, caterpillar, centipede, spider, ant, woodlice, snail, slug).

Preparation

Look around the chosen area and ascertain what wildlife is living there. Place stones and wood in different places to encourage minibeasts. Collect a selection of information books, story books and pictures of minibeasts. Divide the piece of paper into two sections. Write the captions: 'We found this minibeast' and 'Where we found it'.

What to do

Tell the children that different creatures like to live in different places. Encourage the children to think about where they have seen ants, spiders and ladybirds. Suggest that creatures need homes and food as we do.

Encourage the children to be aware of creatures living nearby. Ask the children if they would like to become 'nature spies' and discover which creatures are living nearby and where they have made their homes. Ask them to think about why a ladybird likes to live near plants and shrubs. Do they know who carries their home on their back? How can we protect the creatures and where they live?

Tell the children that they are going on a 'Nature watch'. Take them out to the chosen area. Help them to look for different creatures. Show them how to carefully turn over logs and stones, making sure that they put them back in the same position. Ask them to try and record what creatures they found and where.

When you get back from your walk, gather the children's results together and fill out the prepared piece of paper detailing the things that the children found on their 'Nature watch'.

Discussion

Where do minibeasts live? Do they need different homes? Do we all live in the same sort of houses? Where do other animals live? Tell the children that there are groups of people who help to look after our environment (such as, Friends of the Earth, RSPCA Animal Action Club for children, World Wildlife Fund, Royal Society for the Protection of Birds, [the YOC is the junior branch] – addresses on page 96). Link this with the activity 'A load of rubbish' and 'The park rangers' (pages 51 and 54), and the assembly 'Caring for the countryside' in Chapter 8, (page 65).

Follow-up activities

◇ Use the photocopiable sheet on page 95 to consolidate the activity. Encourage the children to describe the different creatures and their environments.
◇ Repeat the 'Nature watch' activity to see what happens at different times of year, or in different weather conditions.
◇ Write to environmental organisations for their education packs.
◇ Display information, story books and CD-ROMs about creatures.

OLD OR NEW?

Objective

History — To extend children's awareness of the past by examining different buildings and the ways they need to be cared for by a curator.

Group size

Up to six children.

What you need

Ten pictures of old and new buildings, for example, a castle, a block of flats, a thatched cottage, a modern supermarket, a fast food restaurant, a large manor house, a factory, a windmill, a church, a school (a good source are magazines, calendars and newspaper supplements) card, adhesive plastic film, scissors.

Preparation

Mount the pictures on to separate pieces of card and cover with adhesive plastic film. Cut each picture into four horizontally and vertically.

What to do

Mix up the pieces of the pictures and ask the children to make the buildings complete.

When they have finished talk about the differences and similarities between the buildings.

Explain that some of the buildings are old and some are new. Ask the children if they can name any of the buildings. Can they tell you if they are old or new? Compare two of the pictures and encourage the children to describe the differences. Ask the children if they know or have visited any old buildings. Explain the role of the curator and how the buildings are looked after for all of us to enjoy.

Discussion

What would happen to buildings if they were not looked after? Why is it important for the buildings to be cared for? Encourage the children to identify common things about the buildings (doors, roofs, windows). What can the children say about the castle? Do people live there? What is the thatched roof made of? What were windmills used for? How can we tell if something is old or new?

Follow-up activities

✧ Tell the children that people look after old buildings in different ways. Tell them about organisations such as the National Trust.
✧ Arrange a visit to an old building, for example, a church or castle.
✧ Create a 'museum' area in your setting. Collect objects from the past and display these with their modern equivalents (for example, hot water bottles, kitchen utensils, toys, games).
✧ Read the story of the 'Three little pigs'. Ask the children to consider how long the pigs' different homes would last.

CHAPTER 7
DISPLAYS

Displays should reflect not only the children's completed work but should stimulate further learning. They should not be static but changed and added to regularly.

CREATING A DISPLAY

Interactive display

Make opportunities for short and long term displays using different surfaces, for example walls, table tops and cupboards. Include both 2D and 3D presentations in your displays. Use areas throughout the building to stimulate discussion and inform other adults and children about the work your group is doing.

Involve the children in creating the displays ensuring that both adults' and children's work forms the displays. Displays should be interactive— designed to enable children to participate wherever possible. Children should be able to see and handle displays and be encouraged to engage with the objects included.

Captions on all displays are very important and lettering should be bold and clear. Information technology can be used to provide eye-catching captions and labels. Encourage the children to take part in producing them.

Basics for display

A wide selection of materials can be used as display backing. These can include rolls of wallpaper, hessian, lengths of fabric, polystyrene tiles, card and sugar paper in various colours and rolls of boldly coloured frieze paper. Boxes and containers of different shapes and sizes give height to a table or cupboard top display and add a three-dimensional element to a wall display.

Supplement your basic display ingredients with materials such as: wallpaper borders, gift paper, newspapers, pieces of garden trellis, rolls of sequin waste, small pieces of fabric, ribbon, string, pasta, natural objects (dried flowers and leaves), pebbles, stones, waste materials, tulle, felt and corrugated card. Label and store the materials accessibly.

KEEPING US HEALTHY

What you need

An area of wall space and a small table or shelf, a roll of boldly coloured frieze paper, a co-ordinating/contrasting drape, plain white or yellow card and thick felt-tipped pens. A selection of nurses', doctors', and dentists' outfits, coat hangers, a hook. Children's paintings of nurses, doctors, and dentists, a group collage of the health centre, posters about healthy eating, dental care and healthy exercise. Circles of card or PE hoops. A box containing a toy doctor's kit, toothbrushes, toothpaste, dental floss, bandages, adhesive dressings and pretend ointment.

Preparation

Write some labels on the card saying: 'These are things the dentist tells us to use'; 'These are things the doctor uses' and 'These are things the nurse uses'.

What to do

Back the wall with boldly coloured frieze paper. Set up the wall display using the children's paintings, collage and posters. Enlist the children's help. Ask for suggestions for captions and a main heading. Cover the table top or shelf with a drape and place the three set rings in position. Place the box of objects on the table top or shelf. Hang the uniforms on a hook at the side of the display.

Discussion

Gather the children round the display. Familiarise the children with the paintings and posters. Read the three labels for the sets on the table top display. Place each label in a set ring. Focus the children's attention on the box of objects. Ask them to

suggest in which set ring the objects should be placed. Allow the children to take turns to place the items in the correct set.

Show the children the play outfits and discuss who would wear them. Develop the children's observation skills by swapping the labels of the set rings. Ask the children to say what is wrong with the set and match the labels correctly. Put some of the objects into the wrong sets. Can the children recognise the odd one out?
(This display relates to the activities in Chapter 3 'Keeping us healthy'.)

THE GARDEN CENTRE

What you need

A space in the room to create a garden centre. Two small tables, green fabric, trellis, brightly coloured paper, an area of wall space, various boxes, thick felt-tipped pens, staple gun, scissors. A roll of wallpaper borders showing fruit or flowers. Poster or powder paints, seed packets (made by the children), simple stencils of flowers and fruit made from thick card, a selection of different sized plastic plant pots, potting compost, trowels, forks, some silk, plastic or dried flowers, a play cash register, plastic coins and notes, card for labels.

[This is an interactive display related to the activity 'The garden centre' on page 52.]

What to do

Set up the tables and cover with fabric. Expand the trellis and suspend from the ceiling behind the table. Back the display board with brightly coloured paper. Put out the other gardening objects (trowel, potting compost, plant pots, flowers, forks, plant labels). Gather the children round and allow them to look at the display. Encourage them to touch and discuss the objects to be used.

Show the children the wallpaper borders and set up a painting area for children to print and design their own borders using the prepared patterns and stencils. Ask the children to design and label the seed packets.

Invite the children to help you to decide the layout of the garden centre and choose a name for it. Make a large label for the chosen name and a series of captions such as: 'Buy your seeds here'; 'This week's special offer' and 'Pay here'.

Discussion

Gather the children round the display area. Ask them to suggest other objects that might be found at a garden centre. Read out the labels and ask the children to repeat them. Encourage them to make decisions as to where the captions and labels should go. Make extra labels and place them in a folder so that the children can be encouraged to choose and use different labels in their role-play.

FISH FROM THE SEA

What you need

An area of wall space, light and dark blue frieze paper and thin card. Black felt-tipped pens, white paint and a sponge. A length of green tulle, empty frozen fish packets, a piece of firm netting, stiff card, stapler, glue sticks, scissors. Different kinds of coloured paper, old magazines, wrapping paper, kitchen foil, wallpaper, various buttons, sequins or sequin waste, pieces of brightly coloured fabric, poster paints, thick crayons, sugar paper.

What to do

Set up the display board with the light blue frieze paper for the sky, dark blue for the sea and a piece of firm netting as the fishing net. Cut and stick on the green tulle to form the sea bed. Select two or three children to sponge print the waves on the dark blue sea. Allow all the children (in groups) to cut fish shapes from the stiff card and to make collage fish using the various media collected. Encourage the children to stick their fish on to the sea.

Show the children the examples of frozen fish packets. Staple the frozen fish packets to pieces of concertina card and stick all round the top and sides of the display to form a border. Encourage children to recall the different names of the fish. Write the names on fish shaped pieces of card and secure to the bottom edge of the display board. Ask the children to suggest a title for the display.

Discussion

Talk about the sea and sky on the display board. Discuss the various fishes that the children have created. Describe how people who fish go out to sea in trawlers in the very early morning. Explain how the fish are netted and brought back to the port. Explain that some fish are sold fresh and other fish are sent to factories to be frozen and put into packets.

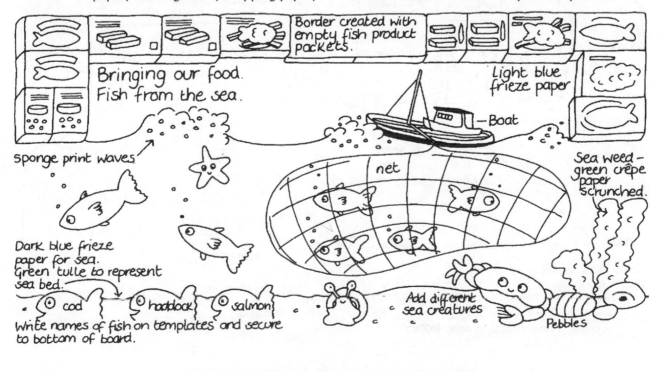

Border created with empty fish product packets.

Bringing our food.
Fish from the sea.

Light blue frieze paper

Boat

sponge print waves

net

Sea weed – green crêpe paper scrunched.

Dark blue frieze paper for sea.
Green tulle to represent sea bed.

cod   haddock   salmon

Write names of fish on templates and secure to bottom of board.

Add different sea creatures

Pebbles

ROAD SAFETY WEEK

What you need

Portable screens or display board, small tables, black sugar paper to cover the tables, drawing pins or staples, staple gun, white paint and brushes, LEGO, light coloured card (to make houses), black felt-tipped pens, thick crayons. Road safety posters and pamphlets, photographs of the children on road safety walks. Play people and small dolls.

(This display can be made portable and used as a backdrop to the road safety assembly (see page 64) or it can be put up more permanently in your room.)

What to do

Mount all the posters, pamphlets and photographs either on the screens or a display board. Ask the children to suggest captions where possible such as: 'Our lollipop lady helps us to cross the road safely', 'Look for a pedestrian crossing' and 'What should you do to cross the road?' Attach these to the screen or display board. Read all the finished captions out together to reinforce the ideas.

Cover the tables with black sugar paper and encourage the children to contribute to the table top model by making the background of houses and shops from card folded in a zigzag. Ask them to use pens or crayons to add detail to the houses.

Paint a zebra crossing and make cars, buses and lorries from LEGO, place some play people and small dolls in the setting.

Discussion

If you are using the display as part of the children's road safety assembly, ask the children to suggest who they could invite to their assembly. Who helps them to learn about crossing the road safely? Discuss the posters, pamphlets and photographs. What do they tell us about road safety?

Invite the children to examine the finished display and consider who else is going to look at the display, discussing the effect it should have in helping promote road safety.

Link this display to the activity 'Road safety' on page 38 in Chapter 4.

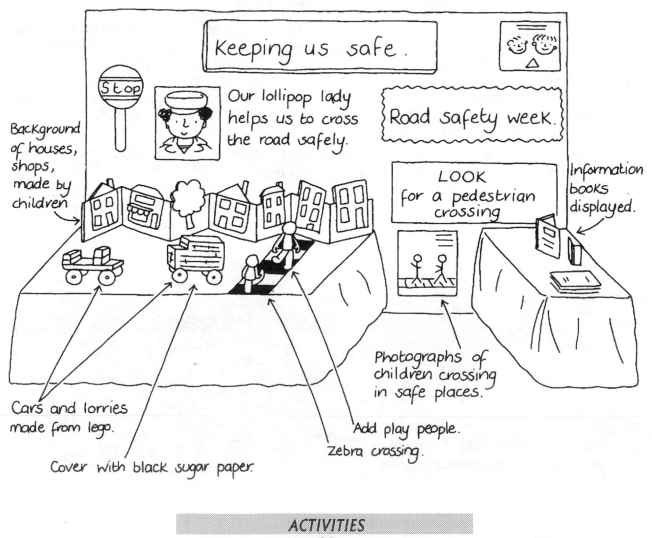

Background of houses, shops, made by children

Cars and lorries made from lego.

Cover with black sugar paper.

Zebra crossing.

Add play people.

Photographs of children crossing in safe places.

Information books displayed.

Keeping us safe.

Our lollipop lady helps us to cross the road safely.

Road safety week.

LOOK for a pedestrian crossing

Stop

CHAPTER 8
ASSEMBLIES

This chapter suggests ideas for assemblies or group sharing times on the theme of 'People who help us' and includes activities, prayers and songs.

PEOPLE WHO HELP US

This assembly could be used as an introduction to the topic or as a 'finale' when the activities in the book have been completed. Either way the essential purposes of assemblies would be served in the sense of gathering together the children, teachers, helpers, family members and friends to share in the life of the group, class or school. Help the children to make invitations for this event and involve them in the planning. Invite members of the community that have shared their expertise with the children (school nurse, fire-fighter, local police officer) to come along and see the children's work.

Introduction

Introduce the assembly by welcoming all those present. Encourage individual children to introduce the 'people who help us' describing the roles that these people play.

What to do

Dress the children in 'helper' outfits, (nurse's, doctor's, police officer, lollipop person). These outfits need only consist of hats.

Make sure the children are sitting facing the audience. Introduce the children according to their roles, (for example, nurse, doctor, fire-fighter). Give a simple explanation of the part they play in helping us. Mention that some helpers do not wear a special uniform. Can the children think who they might be? (Classroom helpers, school secretaries, teachers and so on).

Reflection

Lead the children to consider the people who help us: what might happen if we had nobody to help us?

How can we help at home and school? What kind of helping job would the children like to do when they grow up?

Sometimes people who help us have to stop us doing the things we like to do. They stop us doing things that might be dangerous or bad for us. The nurse or doctor might have to give us injections or medicine to make us feel better when we would rather go out to play with friends. Being good helpers is not always easy.

> ### Prayer
>
> Dear God, We thank you for all the kind people who help to keep us fit and safe and make our lives easier. Help us to help them in any way we can, even if it is hard. Guide us to grow into helpful, caring people ourselves. Amen.

Song

Close the assembly by singing 'Stand up, clap hands, shout thank you Lord' from *Someone's Singing Lord* (A&C Black).

PEOPLE WHO KEEP US SAFE ON THE ROAD

This is an assembly that would fit in with many of the activities in Chapter 4. The focus is on the need to listen carefully and obey instructions. Invite parents and other adults involved in the children's care to this assembly so that they can share the emphasis on road safety with their children. If possible invite a lollipop person and the local road safety officer.

Before the assembly, ask the children to paint large road safety pictures. Display materials purchased from RoSPA (Royal Society for the Prevention of Accidents) in the hall/meeting area.

Introduction

Introduce the assembly by welcoming parents, friends and special visitors. Tell the children an anecdotal story about a boy playing with a football in his garden near the road. He kicked his ball too

hard and it went into the road. He rushed out to fetch it. A car was coming and the driver had to break suddenly to stop. Ask the children about 'safe' play areas in the neighbourhood.

What to do

Ask the children to help act out a road safety play. Place a mock zebra crossing along the front of the room. Ask for a willing adult to participate and choose two children.

The adult and children are walking along a busy road (play a cassette of road traffic sounds). The helper leads the children to the 'crossing' and carries out the road crossing drill: wait until there is a gap in the traffic, look left, look right, look left again and if all the traffic has stopped walk quickly across the road.

Sing the 'road safety' song (to the tune of 'Here we go gathering nuts in May'):

This is the way we cross the road, cross the road, cross the road,
this is the way we cross the road
keeping the safety rules.

Reflection

Draw the children's attention to the fact that roads and streets are not safe places to play. A park or recreation ground is much safer but children should always go with a responsible adult. If you need to cross the road outside school who will help you? Where else is it safe to cross the road? Encourage children to think about travelling safely in cars and buses.

Prayer

Dear God, Thank you for all the people who help to keep us safe on the roads — lollipop people, police officers, road safety officers. Help us to remember that they are trying to keep us safe, to listen to what they say and follow the safety rules. Amen.

Song

Finish by singing, 'Hands to work and feet to run' in *Someone's Singing Lord* (A&C Black).

After the assembly invite the parents and other adults to stay for coffee and a talk on road safety by the road safety officer.

CARING FOR THE COUNTRYSIDE

Children have a natural curiosity and interest in the outdoors and the countryside. This assembly focuses on ways of caring for it. Teach the children the first verse of the poem 'We must protect the countryside' in the Resources section on page 73. Look at each verse of the poem and ask the children to paint pictures to illustrate each aspect of the verses. Write the words of the last verse on a large piece of paper or board.

Before the assembly ensure that the children are well rehearsed. Explain that everybody needs to care about the world in which we live. Give some children the responsibility of holding up their paintings. Choose some other children to dress up as butterflies, trees, flowers, a squirrel and a caterpillar. Encourage them to practise dancing and moving in the manner suited to their costume.

Introduction

Introduce the caring for the countryside theme by asking the children to guess what the assembly is going to be about from the clues you provide, such as: 'There are woods, fields, trees and rivers. People go for walks there. You can go there to listen to the birds and watch insects. Sometimes people drop litter and make it a dangerous place for us and for animals and birds.'

What to do

Start with the children saying the poem 'We must protect the countryside' in the Resources section on page 73. Ask an adult or child to read out or say each verse allowing the children time to stand up and show their painting. The children could all say the final verse with the dressed children standing and moving in a space at the front of the hall/ meeting place.

Reflection

Encourage the children to think about the wonderful world in which we live. Help the children to realise that everybody has a part to play in taking care of the countryside. Encourage children to think of ways they can help. Try and inspire them to have a caring and concerned attitude to the countryside and their immediate environment.

Prayer

Dear God, Thank you for the beautiful world we live in, for the countryside with plants, trees, creatures and flowers. Help us to protect your world so that people will be able to enjoy it as we do. Although we may be small we can still play our part. Thank you for giving us the chance to learn what needs to be done. Help us to remember to do those things which are kind to the world and not destroy the beauty around us. Amen.

Song

Invite the children and adults to sing the hymn 'All things bright and beautiful' in *Come and Praise 1* (BBC).

Collective worship in schools

The assemblies outlined here are suitable for use with children in nurseries and playgroups, but would need to be adapted for use with pupils at registered schools. As a result of legislation enacted in 1944, 1988 and 1993, there are now specific points to be observed when developing a programme of Collective Acts of Worship in a school.

Further guidance will be available from your local SACRE – Standing Advisory Council for RE.

POEMS AND ACTION RHYMES

I'LL HELP TO COOK

I'll help to cook,
I'll help to cook,
I'm looking for a recipe in the big cook book.

Ben wants baked potatoes,
Beryl fancies beans,
Carol goes for carrots,
But Gregory wants greens.

Sue suggests a salad,
Freddy mentions flan,
'Let's have a stew,' says Sammy,
'All in one big pan.'

'Spaghetti is my favourite.'
Stefano sadly sighs,
'Let's have lots of luscious leeks,'
Laura loudly cries.

Wai Sie wants a stir fry,
Felix favours fish,
Krishna says that Korma
Is his very favourite dish.

Kelly calls for coleslaw,
Will wants rice and peas,
Olly orders omelette
Just to be a tease.

I'll help to cook!
I'll help to cook!
I've found a *yummy*
Recipe in the big cook book.

Susanna Kendall

MOVING HOUSE

There's a great big lorry
and it's stopping in the road.
They're letting down the ramp
There'll be lots of things to load.

They're climbing from the lorry
and they're coming to our door.
They're bringing lots of boxes,
yes, more and more and more...!

They're loading up the lorry
with our tables and our chairs.
They've even started taking up
the carpet from the stairs.

They're wrapping up our pictures,
our books and lamps and clocks.
And bit by bit the things we have
get packed into a box.

When everything's been loaded up,
they drive it far away.
And we go driving with them,
for we're moving house today.

Tony Mitton

THE DENTIST

I love to visit my dentist
and read the comics there,
to see his rows of clackety teeth
and ride in his moving chair.

I love to visit my dentist
and stare at his stripy fish,
to see the pink fizz in the glass
and the fillings on the dish.

I love to visit my dentist
and see his tools all gleam,
but when I need a filling...
well, then I'm *not* so keen!

Judith Nicholls

PHOTOCOPIABLE RESOURCES

POSTIE, POSTIE

Postie, postie,
got the pip.
When my dog
gave him a nip.

Postie, postie,
in the snow.
How your ears
and nose do glow.

Postie, postie,
don't be late.
Bring my cards
...then shut the gate.

Postie, postie,
Valentine!
Mary Mousetrap
says she's mine!

Postie, postie,
at the door.
Pile of letters
on the floor.

Postie, postie,
ring the bell.
Wow! Big parcel
from Aunt Nell!

Postie, postie,
thank you for
bringing letters
to my door.

Wes Magee

MY FRIEND BILLY

Let's run, says Billy,
and he runs so fast.
I run, too, but I'm always last.
You can do it, says Billy, just you see...
He's my friend
and he helps me!

Let's climb, says Billy,
and he climbs up high.
I climb, too, I really try.
You can do it, says Billy, just you see...
He's my friend
and he helps me!

I can't swim, says Billy,
and he won't jump in.
I'm splashing in the water up to my chin!
Put on your armbands, Billy, you *can*
swim...
He's my friend
and I'll help him!

Geraldine Taylor

PHOTOCOPIABLE RESOURCES

HAIRCUT

Snip, snap, snickle-snackle,
just a *little* more!
Curls and twirls and tufty bits
scatter on the floor!

Snip, snap, snickle-snackle,
won't my friends all stare!
Dare I, dare I, DARE I look?
Is my head quite bare?

Snip snap, snickle-snackle,
I don't think I dare!
Shall I, shan't I, open eyes?
Is there NOTHING there?

Judith Nicholls

SUPERMARKET SAM

May I help you with the trolley?
Here's a small one for your son!
May I offer you a sample
Of our fresh-baked currant bun?
May I help you reach the yoghurts?
Show you where the baked beans are?
May I help you at the checkout –
Pack your bags and load the car?
HAVE A NICE DAY!

Sue Cowling

THE BIN MEN

Crash and bang and wallop,
the men are here today,
to empty all our rubbish
and cart it all away.

They take it to the rubbish tip,
and there it has to stay,
and the busy, noisy dustmen
come back another day.

It's dirty work for dustmen,
but they whistle and they shout,
and crash and bang and wallop,
so we know when they're about.

Jan Pollard

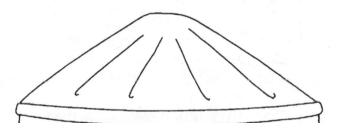

PHOTOCOPIABLE RESOURCES

MY BABYSITTER

My babysitter always cooks
the food I like for my tea.
She lets me watch
my favourite programmes on TV.

My babysitter always reads
my favourite books to me.
My babysitter knows what I like.
She is my gran you see!

John Foster

THE FIREMAN

Up jumps the fireman and slides down the pole
Runs to his clothes that are hanging on the wall
Pulls on his boots, puts his hat on his head
Drives away in the fire-engine, shiny red.

Down jumps the fireman and unrolls the hose
Turns on the tap so the water flows,
Sprays the building quickly, points the hose higher
Top to the bottom, right to left, puts out the fire.

Jillian Harker

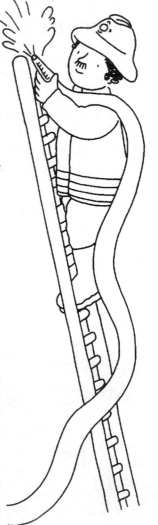

Actions
Children seated. Bell or whistle signals the beginning of the rhyme.
Children jump up, hold hands as if around a pole, go down into a crouched position.
Run several steps, unhook clothes.
Action of putting on boots and hat.
Driving action.
Jump down from cab. Move backwards, unrolling the hose.
Both hands turn on the water tap.
General spraying motion, then pointing the hose upwards.
Movement of hose as in last line or rhyme, followed by mopping brow.

CROSSING THE ROAD

Cars! Buses!
Brrm! Brrm! Brrm!
Lorries! Vans!
Vrrm! Vrrm! Vrrm!

The Lollipop Lady
holds up her pole
and she makes the traffic STOP.
Then we all safely
cross the road
and run to the corner shop.

The Lollipop Lady
wears a big black hat
and her coat has stripes that glow.
When she walks slowly
to the kerb
she lets the traffic GO!

Cars! Buses!
Brrm! Brrm! Brrm!
Lorries! Vans!
Vrrm! Vrrm! Vrrm!

Wes Magee

FARMER

Before the cock crows,
before the sun shows,
the farmer is up and about.

She must feed the new lambs
and tie up the rams
and let Tibbles the farm cat out.

She sets about milking the cows
and then feeding the sows,
there's plenty of work to be done.

There's some feed to be mixed
the tractor needs to be fixed —
there's hardly a moment for fun.

The hen's eggs must be collected,
there's a barn to be erected
and it's now time to harvest the crops.

The sheepdog needs to be fed
before she goes off to bed,
work on the farm never stops.

John Rice

GUESS WHO?

Who's this coming
to your door?
Can you guess?
Are you sure?

Rustle, rustle.
What's that?
A letter landing
on the mat.
Who can that be?

Rattle, rattle.
Clink, clink.
Two fresh bottles
of milk to drink.
What can that be?

On the path —
sound of shoes.
Through the letterbox:
Daily News.
Who can that be?

Did you guess
(were you sure?)
who it was
at your front door?

Tony Mitton

GRANNY

Mum says,
'I'm busy,
so please go and play.'

Sister says,
'I'm reading,
so please go away.'

Dad says,
'Later,
I'm making the tea.'

So I'll go and ask
Granny.
She's always
got time for me.

Tony Mitton

MILKMAN MILLER

Clinkety-clink,
who wants a drink?
Six in the morning
the bottles chink.

Clinkety-clink
who wants tea?
Six in the morning,
one for me!

Clinkety-clink
Who's in that van?
Six in the morning,
Our milkman!

Judith Nicholls

THEMES
for early years

WE MUST PROTECT
THE COUNTRYSIDE

We must protect the countryside –
the flowers and the trees.
We must protect the animals
It's up to you and me.

Don't throw your litter on the ground.
Please put it in a bin,
And close the gate behind you
To keep the cattle in.

Keep your dog upon a lead.
Make sure it doesn't stray.
Stay on the paths. Don't wander
Through the fields of wheat or hay.

Don't leave a broken bottle
Lying on the grass,
Or it could start a fire
Like a magnifying glass.

Don't poke around in birds' nests
Or chase creatures that you see.
Don't pull up plants or flowers
Or break branches off a tree.

Don't squeeze through gaps in hedges,
Please use the stiles or gates.
Don't pollute the water
With rubbish or lead weights.

We must protect the animals,
the trees, the plants, the flowers.
We must protect the countryside.
Remember that it's ours.

John Foster

BAKERY RHYME

Mix the dough, chop the dough
to the right size.
Pop it in a warm place,
Leave the dough to rise.
Plait the dough, shape the dough,
Sprinkle seeds on top.
Bake it in the oven,
Take it to the shop!

Sue Cowling

STORIES

THE STORY OF THE GOOD SAMARITAN

A young man asked Jesus to explain what we must do to please God.

'The law says we must love our neighbour as much as we love ourselves. What does this mean?' he asked. 'Who is my neighbour?'

Jesus told him this story.

One day a man went on a journey from Jerusalem to Jericho. He passed the last house and soon the road curved up into the steep hills. It was very lonely, and there were no other travellers.

Suddenly, a gang of robbers jumped out of the rocks and attacked the man. They took everything he had – even his clothes – and beat him badly. Then they ran away, leaving the man lying by the road, too hurt to move.

Before long, a priest from the Temple came along. He saw the man lying there, but he crossed over the road and hurried quickly past. The robbers might still be nearby!

The next person to come along also worked in the Temple. He too saw the injured man, but like the priest he was afraid to stop, so he hurried past as well.

After a while, a Samaritan came down the road.

Jesus knew how everyone felt about Samaritans. They lived in the next country and believed in different things. No-one would even speak to them.

This Samaritan saw the injured man and felt very sorry for him. He bandaged the man's wounds, then lifted him carefully on to his own donkey and took him down to the nearest inn. He put him to bed and made him comfortable for the night.

The next morning, the Samaritan had to be on his way, so he gave the innkeeper some money and asked him to take care of the injured man until he returned. He promised to pay the innkeeper for any expenses.

'Now,' said Jesus, 'which of those three men do you think really loved the man beaten up by the robbers?'

'The one who took care of him,' replied the young man.

'That's right,' said Jesus. 'God wants us to be kind to *anyone* who needs our help. Not just our friends. If you do this, you will please him very much.'

Jackie Andrews

I'LL DO MY BEST TO HELP

'I want to wear those wonderful stripy trousers on my birthday,' said Jo.

'Into the washing machine with them then,' said Dad.

Five minutes later — a washing machine disaster, water everywhere! Dad phoned the washing machine repairer.

'Can you come quickly, please? We've got problems, and Jo wants to wear those wonderful stripy trousers on her birthday.'

'I'll do my best to help, but my van is being fixed.' The washing machine repairer went round to the garage. 'Can you fix my van quickly, please? I have to mend the washing machine so Jo can wear those wonderful stripy trousers on her birthday.'

'I'll do my best to help,' said the garage mechanic, 'but I have to get a new overall — just look at this one!'

The garage mechanic went to the overall shop. 'Can you find me an overall quickly, please? I have to fix the van so the washing machine repairer can mend the washing machine, so Jo can wear those wonderful stripy trousers on her birthday.'

'I'll do my best to help,' said the overall shop assistant, 'but I'm so hungry I must get a sandwich first.'

The overall shop assistant ran to the café next door. 'Do me a sandwich quickly, love. I have to find an overall so the garage mechanic can fix the van, so the washing machine repairer can fix the washing machine, so Jo can wear those wonderful stripy trousers on her birthday.'

'I'll do my best to help, but I'm waiting for the bread delivery.'

The café owner rang the baker. 'Can you deliver the bread quickly, please? I have to make a sandwich so the overall shop assistant can find an overall, so the garage mechanic can fix the van, so the washing machine repairer can mend the washing machine, so Jo can wear those wonderful stripy trousers on her birthday.'

'I'll do my best to help,' said the baker, 'but I can't get the van out: there's a hole in the road.'

The baker went out to the road menders. 'Can you fill this hole in quickly, please? I have to deliver bread so the café owner can make a sandwich, so the overall shop assistant can find an overall, so the garage man can fix the van, so the washing machine repairer can mend the washing machine, so Jo can wear those wonderful stripy trousers on her birthday.'

'Right away,' said the road menders. 'The stone has just come.'

Then the road menders filled in the hole, the baker delivered the bread, the café owner made the sandwich, the overall shop assistant found the overall, the garage mechanic fixed the van, the washing machine repairer mended the washing machine and Jo *did* wear those wonderful stripy trousers on her birthday — when they were dry, of course.

Susanna Kendall

PLEASE HELP ME FIND MY RABBIT...

On Sunday morning, Tom helped his dad clean out his pet rabbit's hutch. All Ears usually kept still while Tom held her, but this time she wriggled. She wriggled out of Tom's arms, leaped onto the grass and was off like a white rocket, down the garden, round the shed and over the cabbage patch. Tom ran too, and was just in time to see her white tail disappearing under the hedge.

Tom called and called, 'All Ears! Come back! Where are you? Please come back!'

The school playing field was on the other side of the hedge – but it was completely empty.

All day, Tom and his family searched the field for All Ears. Tom wanted to go on looking with a torch all night, but his mum made him go to bed.

On Monday Tom said, 'I'm not going to school. All Ears might come back and I won't be here!'

Dad said, 'I'm glad it's a school day, Tom, because we can ask everyone there to help us find All Ears. I'll take you to school and you'll see...'

'We've lost All Ears,' Dad said to the postman. 'She's our rabbit and she's white and she's all ears.'

'We've lost All Ears,' Dad said to the neighbour at number 5. 'She's our rabbit and she's white and she's all ears.'

Tom was getting the idea. 'We've lost our rabbit,' he told the school crossing lady.

At school, Tom told his teacher, school nurse, the school secretary (who told the Headteacher), the lady who came to help with reading, the dinner ladies – and every single one of his friends. He told the caretaker, who tied a notice to the playground gate.

The whole school was together for singing and to his surprise, the Headteacher called him to the front to talk about All Ears.

'She's snow white,' said Tom 'with pink eyes and when mum first saw her she said "that rabbit's all ears!" And that's her name.'

Soon pictures of All Ears appeared on the walls of the classrooms and Tom's best friend pinned one up in the entrance for the parents to see.

At home time, the school secretary gave all the children a note to take home, asking them to help look for Tom's rabbit.

Everyone wanted to help – and Tom was sure that now All Ears must be found! But that evening the phone didn't ring with good news, and the doorbell was silent. Tom couldn't sleep. He tossed and turned thinking of All Ears shivering and lost.

Tom was up early on Tuesday. He tiptoed to the window and looked out in the moonlight at the empty hutch with it's door left open, just in case All Ears came home.

He heard the clink of milk bottles at the front door and then he heard the milkman talking to himself.

That's odd, thought Tom, I expect he's feeling lonely.

Then the milkman did what he had never done before so early in the morning – he rang the bell. Tom's dad answered. 'I've found a rabbit by the door,' said the milkman, holding the rabbit tightly. 'It's white and it's all ears. I expect it belongs to someone at the school. Can you help me?'

Tom raced downstairs. 'It's All Ears!' he cried. 'You've helped *me*! It's *my* rabbit!'

Geraldine Taylor

SUSIE'S SPECS

'Mummy, the telly's gone funny!' Susie shouted. 'The picture's all blurry!'

'Oh, no, that's all I need,' groaned Susie's Mum, hurrying in. She looked over at the television set and frowned. Then she looked at Susie, who was sitting in a chair in the far corner of the room, rather than on the sofa near the television.

'Susie come and sit on the sofa for a moment, please,' said Mum. She waited for Susie to climb up beside her. 'Is the TV still blurry?'

Susie smiled, 'No, it's fine now. You fixed it!'

'The TV doesn't need fixing,' said Mum. 'But I think you might need glasses. We'd better pay a visit to the optician's.'

Susie's dad wore glasses, so did Gran, and Simon in nursery school. So Susie wasn't worried about that. But she was worried about going to the optician. What would happen?

The next day they went along for their appointment.

First, a man asked Susie and her mum some questions, and then they were shown into a bright little room where a friendly lady in a white coat asked them to sit down. She picked up a funny pair of glasses.

'I'd like you to put these on for me, please, Susie,' she said.

Susie looked at them in horror. They were awful: big and heavy with funny lenses. She couldn't wear those!

'I don't want to wear those! I want some proper glasses like Simon's!' she told Mum, almost crying.

Mum and the optician laughed. 'Don't worry, Susie, you don't have to wear *these*. I just want you to put them on now so I can find out what sort of lenses you need.'

Susie was relieved about that! She put on the funny glasses and the optician kept slotting in different lenses until Susie told her she could see better.

'Right that's it,' smiled the optician, taking the funny glasses off Susie. 'Now we know what kind of lenses to make you. Would you like to go and choose your frames?'

There were a great many frames on display: round, square, oval, silver, gold and different colours. Susie seemed to try them all. At last she chose a shiny blue pair. She looked at herself in the mirror and smiled happily.

'You look lovely,' said Mum. 'Very nice,' said the optician. 'Can I wear them now?' asked Susie. The optician smiled. 'We have

to put the lenses in first,' she said. 'If you come back tomorrow they'll be ready for you.'

Susie could hardly wait! She told Dad all about the trip to the optician's that night and how she thought she had to wear the funny glasses. 'That's what I thought when I first went to the opticians!' laughed Dad.

The next day, Susie and Mum went to fetch her glasses. Susie put them on straight away. Everything looked really bright and clear. As soon as she got home, she switched on the television and sat on the chair again in the corner of the room.

'You're right, Mum,' she said, 'the telly doesn't need fixing. And neither do my eyes, now!'

Karen King

ALICE AND TOM FIND THE WAY

Life had been very exciting lately for five-year-old Tom and his sister, Alice, who was nearly seven. They had moved to a new house, which had a bigger garden than their old one. *And* they were going to a new school, which they liked very much. *And* Mum would soon be going to work in a shop in town on Thursdays and Fridays!

Tom was very worried about Mum going to work. 'Who will look after us?' he asked in a shaky voice. 'Gran and Grandad live too far away!' Alice didn't say anything. She guessed that someone would be coming to look after them and take them to school on the days Mum had to go to work, and hoped it would be someone they liked.

Emma was fun. She wore flowery leggings, a bright red T-shirt and green trainers. She brought her own little Teddy with her, too, and said that he went everywhere with her, even though she was a grown-up person! By the time she left them that evening. Tom and Alice had decided that she was the best child-minder anybody could possibly have. They looked forward to seeing her again.

On the first day that Emma was to take them to school, Alice and Tom waited impatiently for the doorbell to ring. They were so excited. So when Emma arrived, they nearly knocked each other over in their hurry to open the door.

Mum gave her a little pile of notes telling her things she needed to know, then they all went to the door to wave while Mum got in the car and drove away.

Emma looked at the notes. 'Well, the first note is a map showing me the way to your school.' she said.

'Is it a map of Africa?' asked Tom. 'I don't want to go there today.'

The children thought it was great fun following a map. (Mrs Jones looked at the map too, and had an idea for a special lesson.)

They soon reached the school gates. Emma gave Alice and Tom a big hug as they went inside, and everyone waved goodbye to her.

That morning, Mrs Jones talked to her class about Alice, Tom and Emma following their map to find the way to school and the special landmarks they looked for. She asked all the children to draw four places that they passed on *their* way to school and — of course — Alice managed this better than all of them!

Janet Morris

SONGS

FIREMAN FRED

1. Who's going to put the flames out? Fire-man Fred. Who's going to put the flames out? Fire-man Fred. With his
2. Who's going to drive the en-gine? Fire-man Fred. Who's going to drive the en-gine? Fire-man Fred. With its

buck-et and his hose and his yel-low fire-man clothes. He's going to put the fi-re out.
lad-der and its light it has got a fire to fight. He's going to put the fi-re out.

Clive Barnwell

MEET MY DENTIST (WHAT A NICE MAN)

Lazy calypso
Chorus:

Meet my den-tist, what a nice man, He'll make you smile if an-y-one can.

1. O-pen wide, let's look in-side. Clean and white, well that's al-right.

David Moses

GUESS WHO?

Hazel Hobbs

2. Guess who this is right behind the chair,
Right behind the chair,
Right behind the chair,
Washing, brushing, snipping at my hair.
Right behind the chair
(spoken) It's the hairdresser (or barber/
stylist etc.).

3. Guess who this is looking at my teeth,
Looking at my teeth,
Looking at my teeth.
Shines a light right in and underneath,
Looking at my teeth
(spoken) It's the dentist.

4. Guess who this is rattling down the
street,
Rattling down the street,
Rattling down the street.
Takes the rubbish, makes the dustbin neat.
Rattling down the street
(spoken) It's the bin man (or refuse disposal
person etc.).

5. Guess who this is checking all the food,
Checking all the food,
Checking all the food.
Bread and fruit and meat that can be stewed.
Checking all the food
(spoken) It's the cashier (or check-out
person etc.).

6. Guess who this is listening to my chest,
Listening to my chest,
Listening to my chest.
Checks my pulse and gives my eyes a test.
Listening to my chest
(spoken) It's the doctor.

> *Try adding mimes to demonstrate
> the activities described in the song
> words. The last line of each verse
> is in spoken form to allow for
> flexibility of gender names or local
> terms to describe the occupations.*

THE WHEELIE BIN SONG

Solo: "I'm Fred wheel-ie bin, I'm wait-ing in the row," And the man in the van says "Quick as you can! There are nine more wheel-ie bins to go!"

go!"

Ann Bryant

Have ten children in a row. They take turns to sing the solo tune, inventing a name for the wheelie bin each time. The class changes 'nine more wheelie bins' to eight, then seven and so on as each soloist sits down.

WHOSE HAT IS THAT?

Like a barn dance

Caller: Whose hat is that? Whose hat is that? Tell me please.

G **C** **G** **Am** **D** **G** **C** **G** **D7**

1. That's the hat of the farm - er, It's big and broad and_ flat, There's mud on the top and the brim goes flop.

Chorus:
G **Am** **D7** **G** **D.C.**

That's how we know, That's how we know, That's how we know the hat.

Music — Gillian Parker

2. That's the hat of the fireman
   It's really yellow and fat
   It shines like marge
   And it's ever so large.

Chorus: That's how we know etc.

3. That's the hat of the nurse
   A small white cap is that
   It's nice and neat
   With a careful pleat

Chorus: That's how we know etc.

*(Other verses can be made up by pupils
and teachers to the same pattern.)*

Words — Trevor Millum

MILKMAN

Early in the morning there's a very special man,
Up to every door he comes in rain or snow or sun,

Calling at the houses with his clink-y, clank-y van.
Leaving bottles full of cream-y milk for every-one.

Milkman, Milkman, leave some milk for me, I need some for my cereal, I need some for my tea.
Milkman, Milkman, happy I will be if you will come tomorrow and will leave some milk for me.

Clive Barnwell

THE DRIVER OF OUR SCHOOL BUS

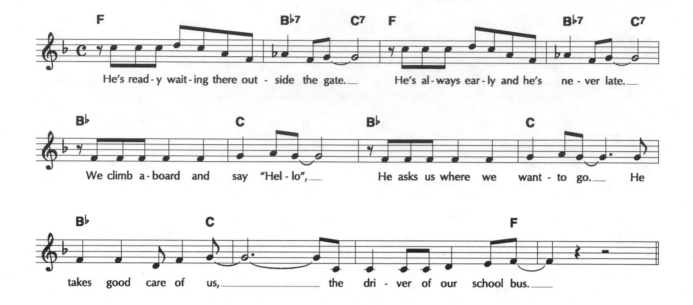

He's read-y wait-ing there out-side the gate. He's al-ways ear-ly and he's ne-ver late. We climb a-board and say "Hel-lo", He asks us where we want-to go. He takes good care of us, the dri-ver of our school bus.

Debbie Campbell

2. He's always cheerful as he drives along
   He likes to whistle as we sing a song.
   He always knows the way to go
   He takes it steady, nice and slow.
   He's never in a rush,
   The driver of our school bus.

FRIENDS AND NEIGHBOURS

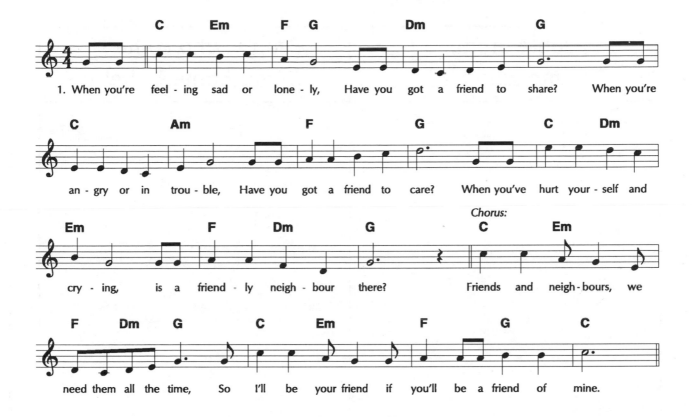

1. When you're feel-ing sad or lone-ly, Have you got a friend to share? When you're an-gry or in trou-ble, Have you got a friend to care? When you've hurt your-self and cry-ing, is a friend-ly neigh-bour there?

Chorus:

Friends and neigh-bours, we need them all the time, So I'll be your friend if you'll be a friend of mine.

Carole Henderson Begg

2. When you need to talk to someone
Have you got a friend to share?
When you need a hug and cuddle
Have you got a friend to care?
When you need some help with something
Is a friendly neighbour there?

Chorus

3. When you want to tell a secret
Have you got a friend to share?
When you're bubbling with excitement
Have you got a friend to care?
When someone needs a helping hand
Are you that neighbour there?

Chorus

Helping in my home

Name _____

People in my home who help	People who come to my home to help

THEMES
for early years

Name _____

Alice and Tom's journey to school

Draw a line to help Alice and Tom find the way.

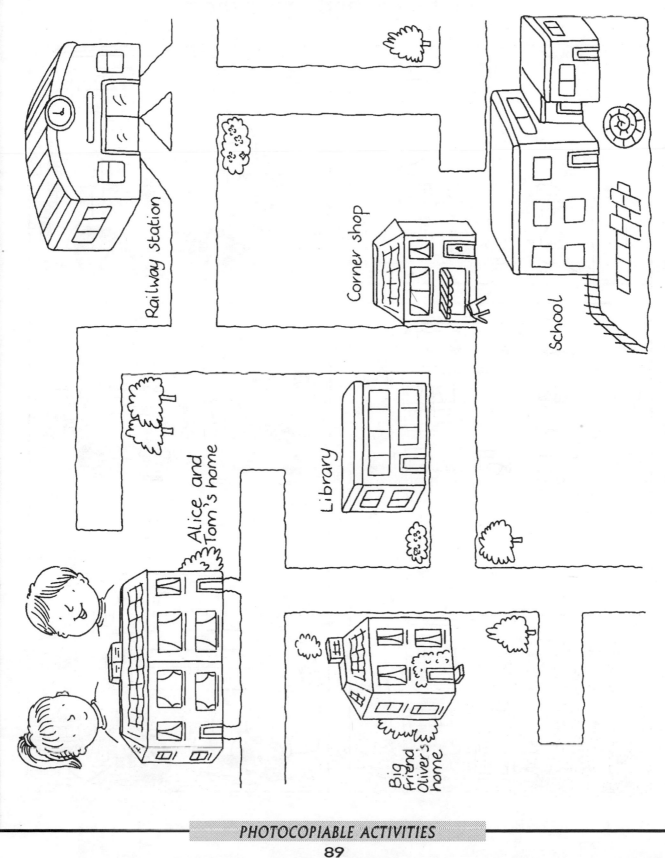

THEMES *for early years*

Moving house

Cut out the pictures, stick them in the right order and colour them in.

My healthy meal

Draw a healthy meal onto this plate.

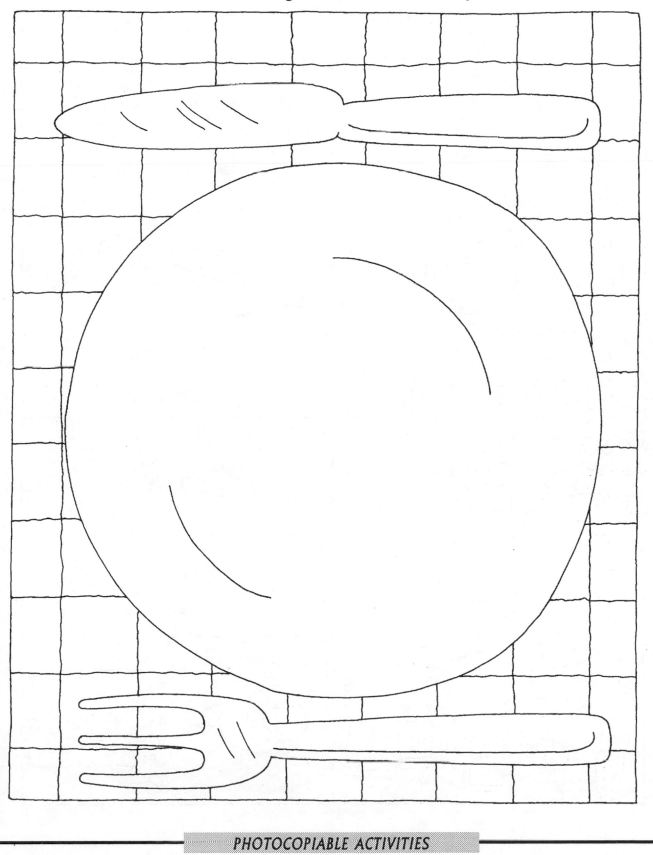

THEMES
for early years

Keeping us healthy

Cut out the pictures and match the objects to the people.

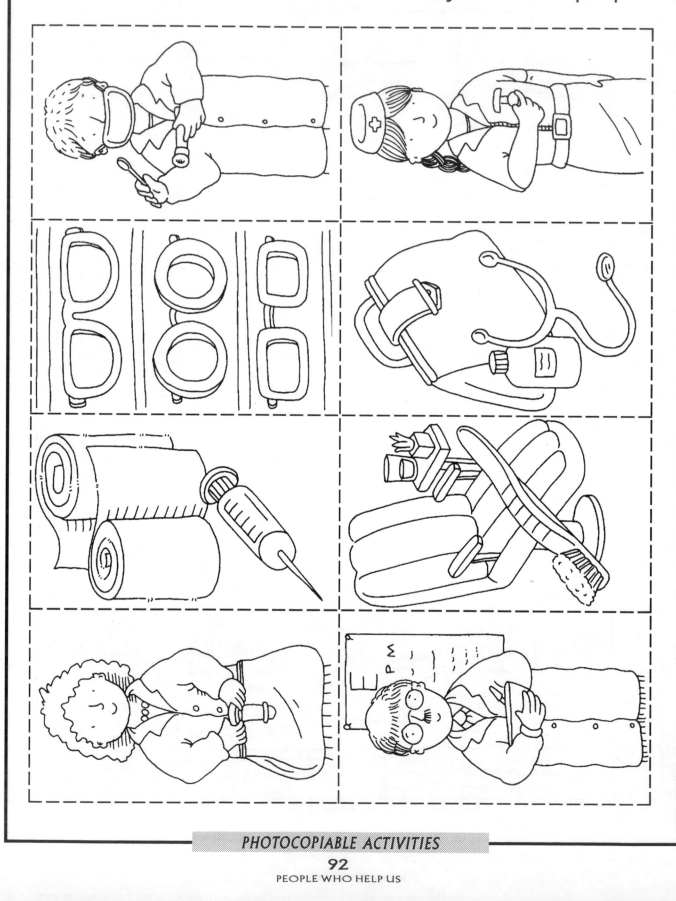

THEMES
for early years

The shopkeeper

Match the objects to the people.

milk deliverer

farmer

fisher

baker

Name _____

At the garden centre

Join up the dots to find the object in the garden centre.

THEMES
for early years

Name _____

Nature watch

Look carefully at the pictures to see who is hiding there.

RECOMMENDED MATERIALS

SONGS
'The fireman' from *Apusskidu* (A&C Black)
'Posting letters' from *Count Me In, Songs and Rhymes about Numbers* (A&C Black)
'Lollipop man' from *Flying Around* (A&C Black)
'Harvest' *from Harlequin* (A&C Black)
'Can you tell me?' from *Okki-Tokki-Unga Action Songs for children* (A&C Black)
'Oh Mr Policeman' from *Silly Aunt Sally* (Ward Lock Educational)
'Milk bottle tops and paper bags' and 'The farmer comes to scatter the seed' from *Someone's Singing Lord* (A&C Black)
Songs from *Tinderbox* (A&C Black) including: 'Poor child', 'Gardens', 'City beasts', 'The tidy box', 'Let it be', 'I've just moved into a new house' and 'I went to the cabbages'.

POEMS AND RHYMES
'Visit to the dentist' by V. Bloom in *Another Second Poetry Book* (OUP)
'The fish with the deep sea smile' by M. Wise-Brown in *A Cup of Starshine* (Walker Books)
'Funny the way different cars start' by D. Baruch in *Machine Poems* (OUP)
Poems from *Poems for the Very Young* by Michael Rosen (Kingfisher) including: 'The Dustman', 'The Barber' and 'The Window Cleaner'.
'Traffic Lights' by J. Foster in *A Red Poetry Paint Box* (OUP)

INFORMATION BOOKS
A Busy Day at the Factory P. Dupasquier (Walker)
Doing the Garden S. Garland (Bodley Head)
Doing the Washing S. Garland (Bodley Head)
Going Shopping S. Garland (Bodley Head)
Look Around You (ed.) A. Cooper (Wayland)
Books from the Macdonald Starters Series: *Fire, Milk, Teeth, Post, Farm, Food* (Out of print)
My Visit to the Dentist D. Bentley (Wayland)
Books from the *Teamwork Series,* 'Post Office', 'Building Site', 'Hospital', 'Police Service', 'Fire Service' (Wayland Publishers)
Books from the *People and Places Series* (Franklin Watts) including: *Farm* by J. Colerne and *Supermarket* by T. Wood. (Out of print)
Shops and Markets Around the World A. Cooper (Wayland Publishers)

PICTURE AND STORY BOOKS
Fireman Sam Series (Buzz Books)
Happy Families (sixteen titles about various roles) Allan Ahlberg (Puffin)
Miss Polly had a Dolly K. Bryant (Mole)
Mrs Molly's Shopping Trolley Trish Cooke (Harper Collins)
Mrs Mopple's Washing line Anita Hewett (Random House)
Mums Don't Get Sick M. Hafner (Walker)
Poor Monty Anne Fine (Mammoth)
Helping Hands, Who's Minding the Store?, Special Delivery, A Quiet Day, all by J. Austen (Story Store, Sapling for Carlton)
Teddy Bears' Moving Day Susanna Gretz (A&C Black)
Topsy and Tim Series J and G Anderson (Blackie)
When I Grow Up I Want To Be D. Hunt Newton (Walker Books)

ADDRESSES AND OTHER RESOURCES
Farm Floor Puzzle, Orchard Toys
The Farm, Infant Software (Sherston Software)
Happy Families Card Game (Waddingtons)
'People who help us' K. Cox and P. Hughes
History from Photographs Series (Wayland)
Cambridge Reading, Talking Books *I went to school this morning* (Sherston Software)
Let's Visit the Farm (Photocopiable activities linked to the Farm, Sherston Software)
Peek-a-Boo Around Our Town, Infant Software (Sherston Software)
Royal National Lifeboat Institution, West Quay Road, Poole, Dorset BH15 1HZ (Tel: 01202 663000)
RSPB, The Lodge, Sandy, Bedfordshire SG19 2DL (Tel: 01767 680551)
Catalogue of resources available from: RSPCA Education, Causeway, Horsham, West Sussex RH12 1HG (Tel: 01403 264181)
Catalogue of resources available from: RoSPA, Edgbaston Park, 353 Bristol Road, Birmingham B5 7ST (Tel: 0121 248 2000)